Power Maths

Year 2 Textbook 2A

Series Editor: Tony Staneff

C000152415

Dexter
Dexter is determined.
He tries hard and never gives up.

flexible

Flo

curious

Ash

brave

Astrid

helpful

Sparks

Contents

This shows us what page to turn to.

Let's start our maths journey!

3

How to use this book

Let's see how Power Maths works!

These pages help us get ready for a new unit.

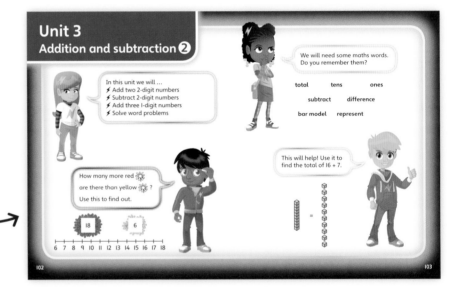

Discover

Lessons start with Discover.

Have fun exploring new maths problems.

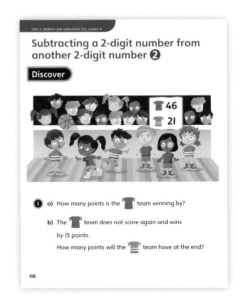

Share

Next, we share what we found out.

Did we all solve the problems the same way?

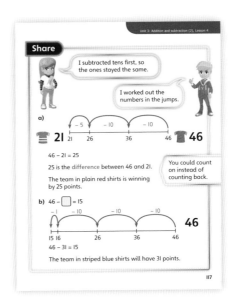

Think together

Then we have a go at some more problems together.

We will try a challenge too!

This tells you which page to go to in your Practice Book.

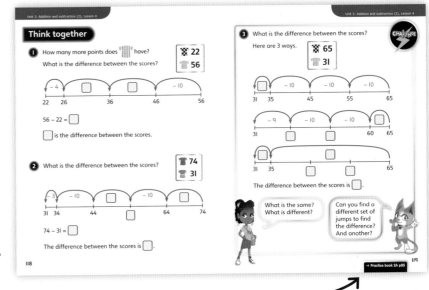

At the end of a unit we will show how much we can do!

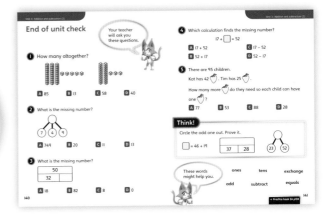

Unit 1
Numbers to 100

In this unit we will ...
- ⚡ Count numbers to 100
- ⚡ Use different ways to show numbers to 100
- ⚡ Use place value grids to make and compare numbers
- ⚡ Count in 10s
- ⚡ Compare and order numbers to 100
- ⚡ Count in 2s and 5s

Do you remember how to use this to find how many there are?

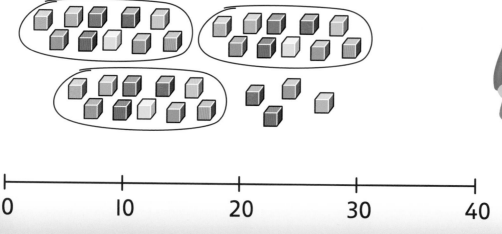

Here are some maths words you have seen before. Which ones can you remember?

tens   ones

place value grid   partition   more

fewer   fewest

greatest   smallest

We can use

Tens	Ones

to show a number. Use it to show 43.

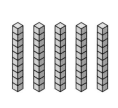

Tens	Ones

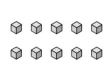

7

Counting objects to 100

Discover

1 **a)** How many ☐ are there?

b) Emma finds 2 more ☐.

How many ☐ are there now?

Share

I will count the blocks one by one.

I will find groups of 10.

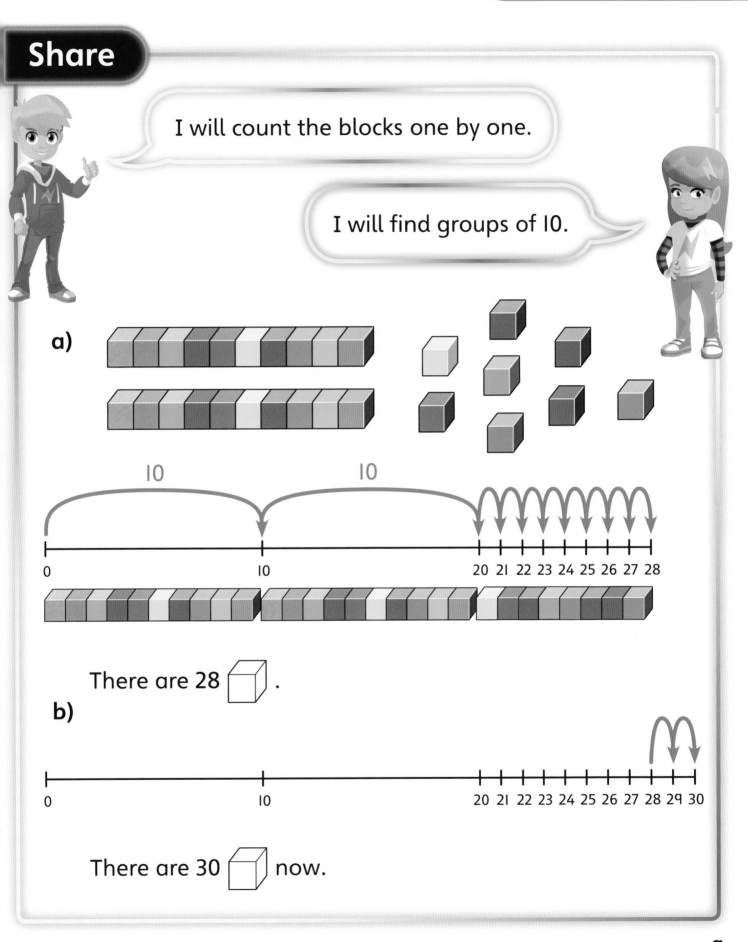

a)

10   10

0   10   20 21 22 23 24 25 26 27 28

There are 28 ▢.

b)

0   10   20 21 22 23 24 25 26 27 28 29 30

There are 30 ▢ now.

Think together

1 How many stars are there?

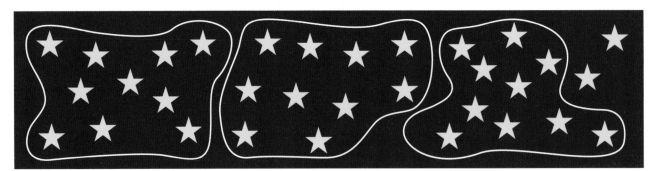

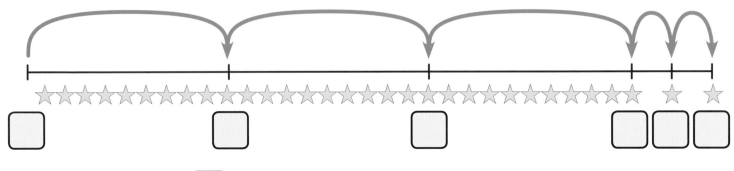

There are ▢ stars.

2 How many cubes are there?

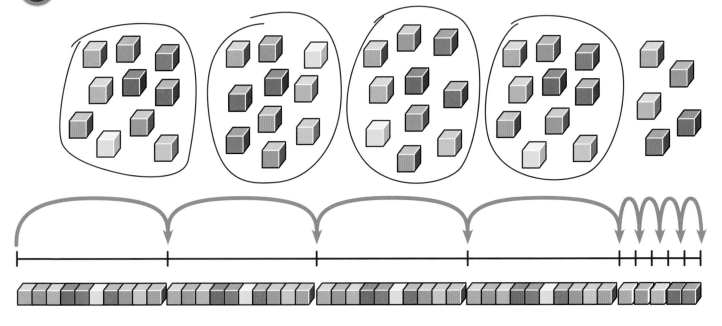

There are ▢ cubes.

3 Emma and Jim have some .

There are 25 seashells.

I think there are 27 seashells.

Prove they are both wrong.

I will check the groups of 10.

11

Representing numbers to 100

Discover

1 a) There are 10 ⌂ in each stack.

How many ⌂ are there in total?

b) The teacher finds 4 more ⌂.

How many are there now?

Share

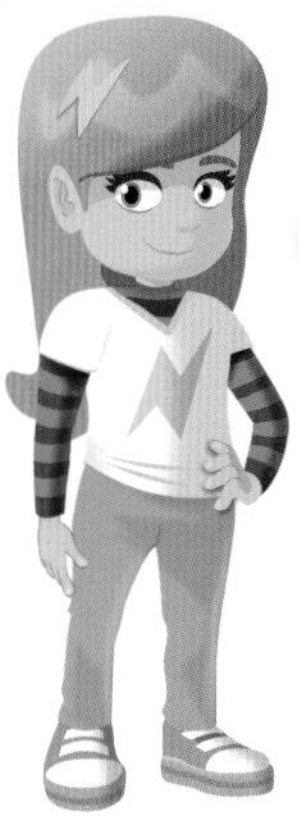

I counted the stacks of 10 △.

I used ⬚⬚⬚⬚⬚⬚ to represent tens.

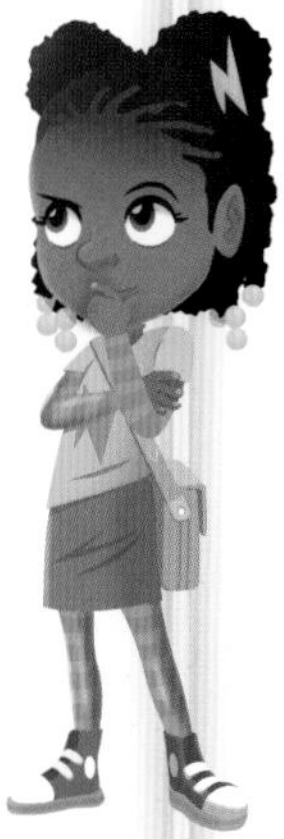

a)

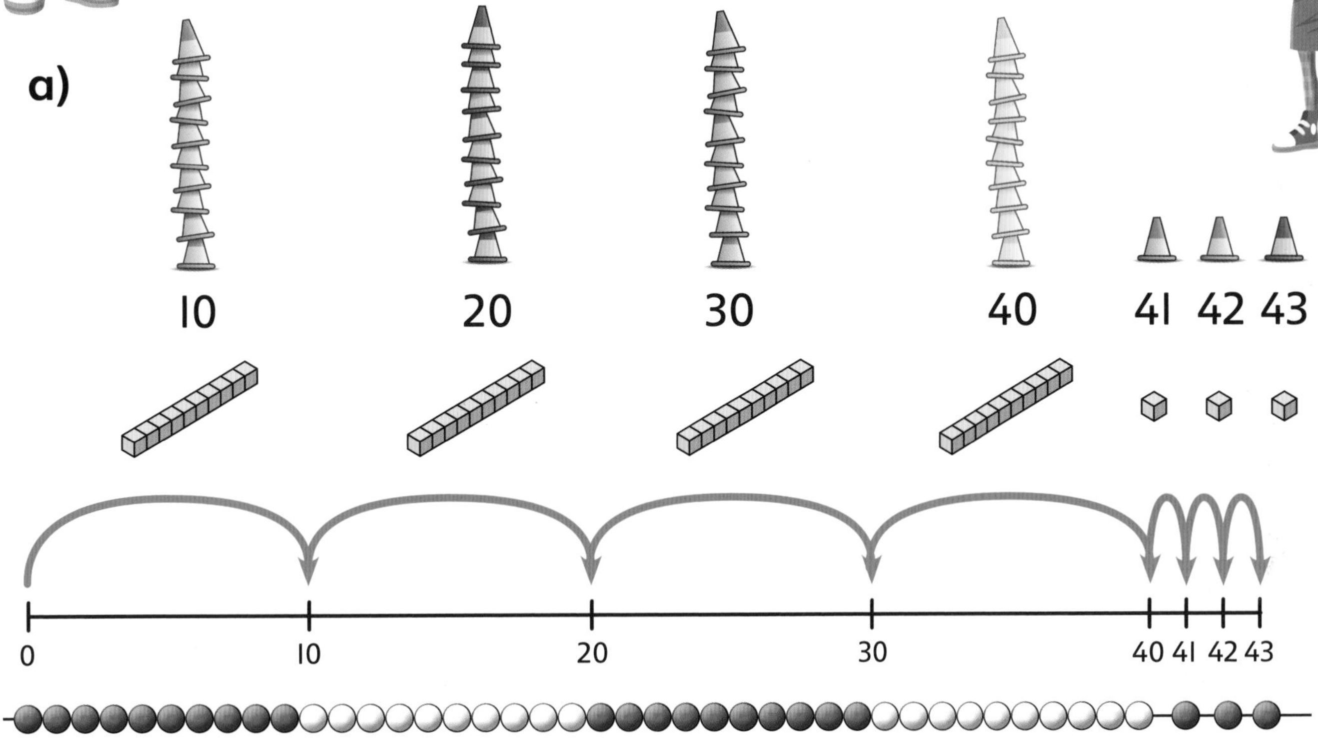

10   20   30   40   41 42 43

There are 43 △.

b)

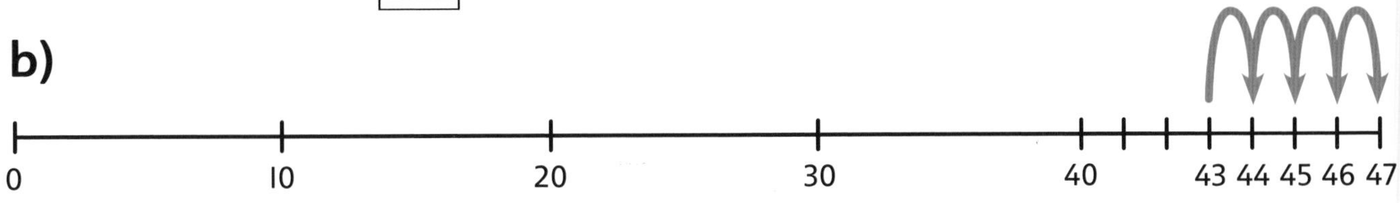

There are 47 △ now.

Think together

1 How many red stickers are there?

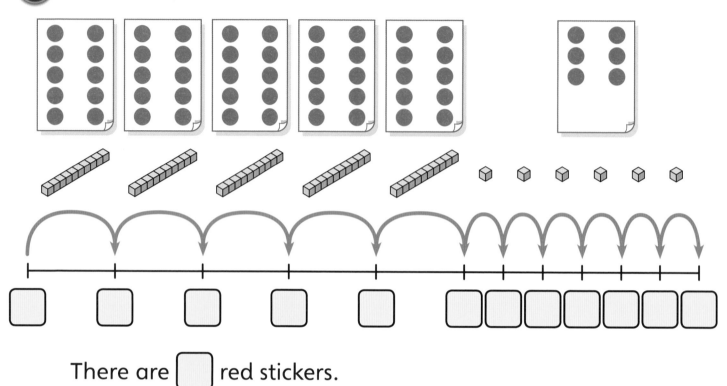

There are ☐ red stickers.

2 There are 10 straws in a  .

Choose the correct number for each group.

Choose from: 33 53 73

a)

b)

c)

3 **a)** What number do these represent?

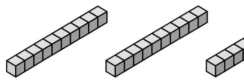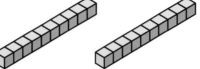

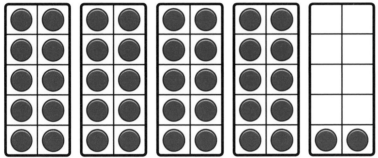

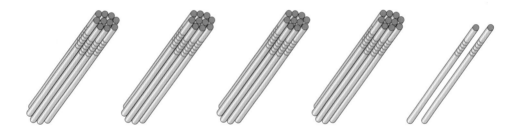

b) Show the number 32 using pictures and equipment.

I can show the number 32 in three different ways.

15

Tens and ones ①

Discover

① **a)** Simon needs 46 pencils.

How many [10 pencils] does he need?

How many ✏ does he need?

b) Molly needs 31 pens.

How many [10 pens] does she need?

How many ✒ does she need?

Share

I will count out the pencils and pens.

I will use  .

a)

 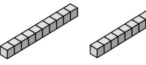 

46 is 4 tens and 6 ones.

Simon needs 4 . He needs 6 .

b)

 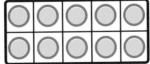 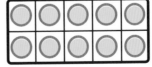 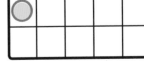

Molly needs 3 . She needs 1 .

17

Think together

1 **a)** Simon needs 56 pens.

How many does he need?

How many  does he need?

56 is ⬚ tens and ⬚ ones.

Simon needs ⬚ 10 pens .

He needs ⬚ ✏️ .

b) Simon needs 32 rubbers.

How many 10 rubbers does he need?

How many 🧼 does he need?

32 is ⬚ tens and ⬚ ones.

Simon needs ⬚ 10 rubbers .

He needs ⬚ 🧼 .

2 Copy and complete the sentences.

a)

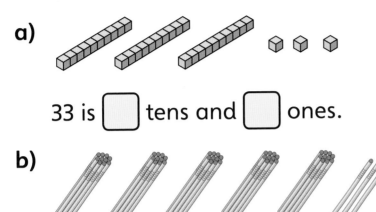

33 is ⬜ tens and ⬜ ones.

b)

53 is ⬜ tens and ⬜ ones.

c)

3	6

⬜ is 3 tens and 6 ones.

3 Who is correct?

Alfie says: "50 is 50 tens and 0 ones."

Bella says: "50 is 5 tens and 0 ones."

Cara says: "50 is 5 tens and 50 ones."

Dev says: "50 is 0 tens and 50 ones."

I made 50 from  .

→ **Practice book 2A p12**

Tens and ones ②

Discover

1 **a)** Show 56 using equipment.

   Write an addition.

   b) What do you need to change to show 46?

Share

I will write 56 as tens and ones first.

I will use a part-whole diagram.

a)

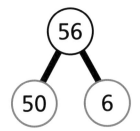

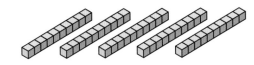

You can partition 56 into 50 and 6.

$56 = 50 + 6$

b)

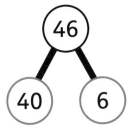

The ones stay the same.

The tens change.

$56 = 50 + 6$

$46 = 40 + 6$

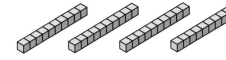

Think together

1 Show 35 using equipment.

Write an addition.

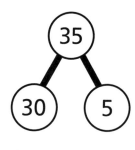

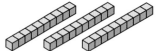

☐ + ☐ = 35

2 Make these numbers using equipment.

Copy and complete the part-whole diagram and addition for each number.

a)

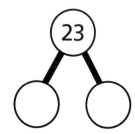

23 = ☐ + ☐

b)

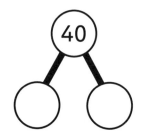

40 = ☐ + ☐

Copy and complete the addition for each number.

c)

2 4

☐ = ☐ + ☐

d)

3 9

☐ = ☐ + ☐

3 Here are 4 part-whole diagrams.

Find the missing numbers.

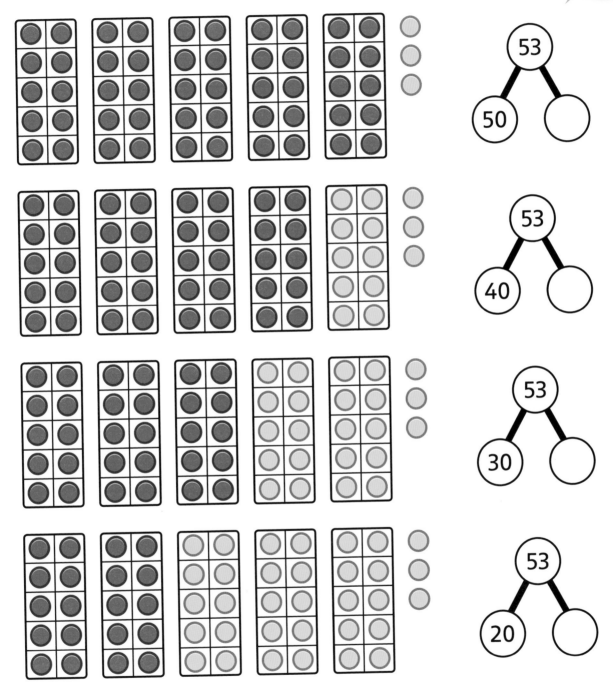

What is the same about the diagrams?

What is different about the diagrams?

→ Practice book 2A p15

Representing numbers on a place value grid

Discover

I a) What is Mr Taylor's number?

b) What is Mia's number?

Share

I will put  into a place value grid.

a) Mr Taylor's number has 3 tens and 2 ones.

Tens	Ones
3	2

Mr Taylor's number is 32.

b) Mia's number has 6 tens and some ones.

Tens	Ones
6	2

62 has 6 tens and 2 ones.

Mia's number is 62.

Can Mia's number be 60?

25

Think together

① Rav chooses one of these numbers:

31, 35, 42, 51, 57, 65, 69

He says: "My number has some tens and 5 ones."

What is Rav's number?

There are two possible answers.

Tens	Ones
	5

Tens	Ones
	5

② Complete the place value grids. Count the cubes carefully.

a)

Tens	Ones

c)

Tens	Ones

b)

Tens	Ones

d)

Tens	Ones

3 Mia has six cards.

| 2 | 0 | 2 | 2 | 5 | 5 |

She makes three different numbers using the cards.

Tens	Ones
2	0

Tens	Ones
2	2

Tens	Ones
5	5

Make three more numbers using the cards.

Tens	Ones

Tens	Ones

Tens	Ones

I made 02. I'm not sure that's a number!

02 means no tens and 2 ones, so I think 02 is the same as 2.

27

→ Practice book 2A p18

Comparing numbers ❶

Discover

1 **a)** Who has more ?

   b) Anna gives to Matt.

   Who has more now?

Share

I will count them all.

I will put the  in rows of 10.

a)
10
20
30
40
50
60
63

10
20
30
40
50
60
70

Compare the last row.

70 is greater than 63.

70 > 63

Anna has more .

b)

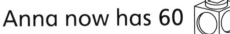

Anna gives 10 away.

Anna now has 60 .

Matt now has 7 tens and 3 ones.

Matt now has 73 .

73 > 60

Matt has more now.

29

Think together

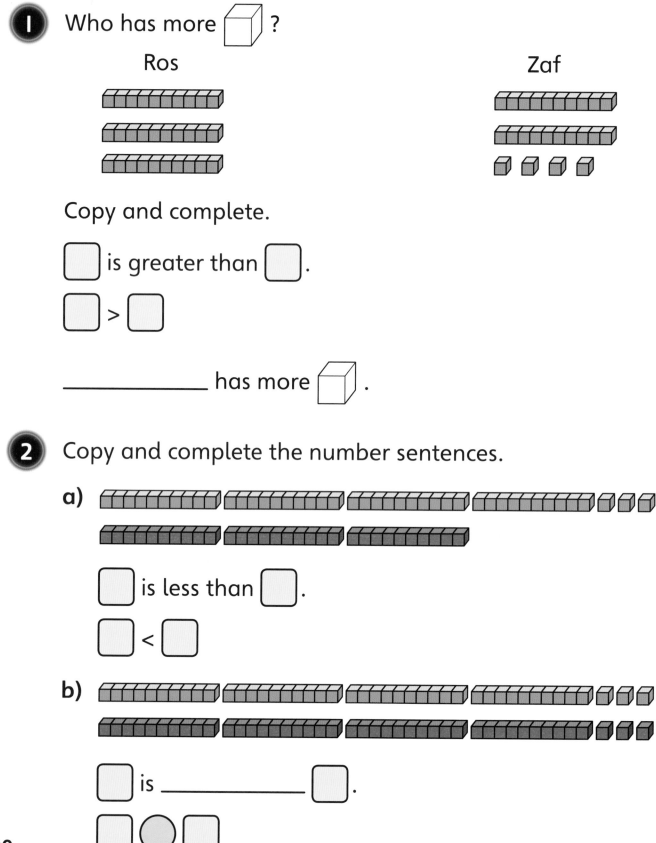

1 Who has more ☐ ?

Ros

Zaf

Copy and complete.

☐ is greater than ☐ .

☐ > ☐

_____ has more ☐ .

2 Copy and complete the number sentences.

a)

☐ is less than ☐ .

☐ < ☐

b)

☐ is _____ ☐ .

☐ ◯ ☐

3 Copy and complete the number sentences.

a)

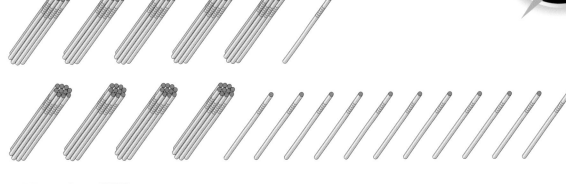

b)

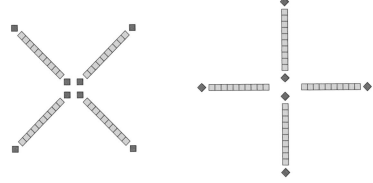

Write <, > or = in the ◯.

If the tens are the same, I can compare the ones.

31

→ Practice book 2A p21

Comparing numbers ❷

Discover

1 **a)** Who has more , Asif or Beth?

b) Dana has 48 and Finn has 53 .

Who has fewer ?

Share

I matched 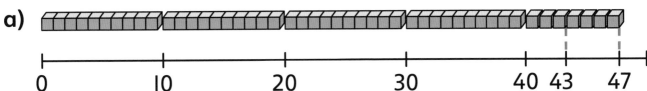 to a number line.

If I use a place value grid, I can see the tens are the same and I can compare the ones.

a)

```
0        10       20       30       40 43    47
```

47 is further from 0, so 47 > 43.

Tens	Ones
4	3

Tens	Ones
4	7

7 > 3 so

47 > 43

Beth has more .

b)

Tens	Ones
4	8

Tens	Ones
5	3

```
0                               40      48 50 53
```

48 < 53

Dana has fewer .

4 tens is less than 5 tens, so we don't need to compare the ones.

Think together

1   **a)**   Tom has 32 . Alexa has 42 .

Who has more ?

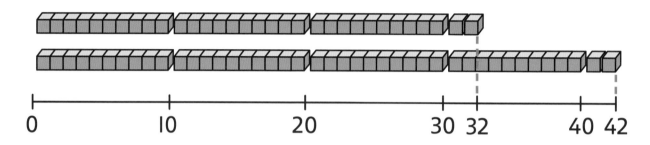

_____ has more .

b)   Oli has 65 . Kia has 62 .

Who has more ?

Tens	Ones
6	5

Tens	Ones
6	2

_____ has more .

2 Copy and complete the number statements.

Use <, = or >.

a) 49 99

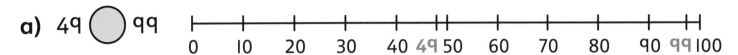

b) 55 50

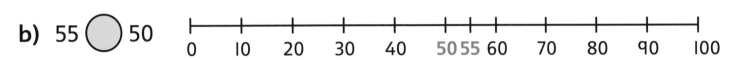

3 Use < = or > to compare the numbers.

CHALLENGE

a)
Tens	Ones
6	4

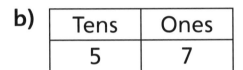

Tens	Ones
2	6

b)
Tens	Ones
5	7

Tens	Ones
7	0

c)
Tens	Ones
6	2

Tens	Ones
6	6

I can tell which is greater just by looking at the tens.

I wonder if that always works.

35

Ordering numbers

Discover

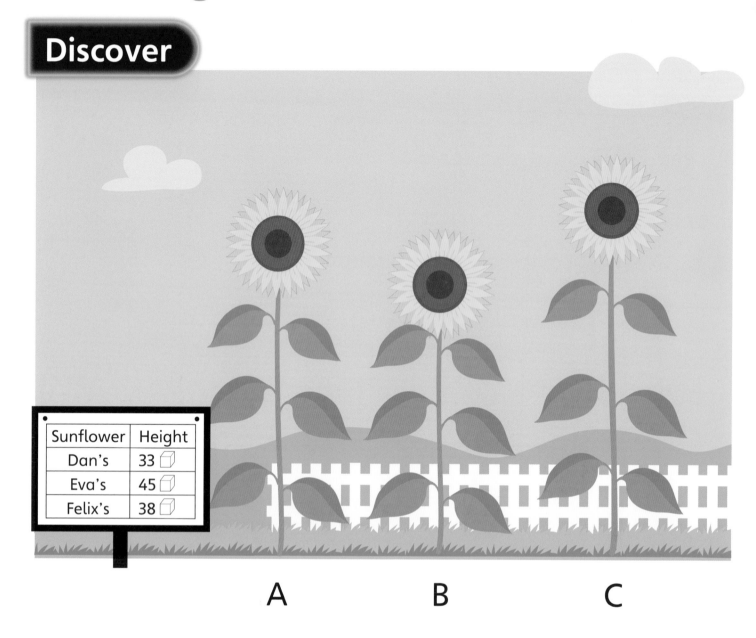

Sunflower	Height
Dan's	33 ⬜
Eva's	45 ⬜
Felix's	38 ⬜

A   B   C

1 Dan, Eva and Felix are using cubes to measure the height of their sunflowers.

a) Whose 🌻 is whose?

b) Write the heights of the 🌻 in order, shortest to tallest.

Share

I will compare the tens and ones.

I will make the numbers using  .

a)

 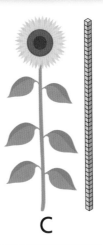

A   B   C

Felix's	
Tens	Ones
3	8

Dan's	
Tens	Ones
3	3

Eva's	
Tens	Ones
4	5

45 has the most tens, so it is the greatest number.

The tallest , C, is Eva's.

3 is less than 8 and so 33 < 38

The shortest , B, is Dan's.

So A is Felix's.

b)

Shortest		Tallest
B	A	C
33cm	38cm	45cm

Think together

a) Which jar contains the fewest buttons?

Tens	Ones

6	7

Tens	Ones
3	1

Tens	Ones
6	3

b) Find the greatest number of buttons.

c) Copy and complete to write the numbers in order.

Greatest　　　Smallest

☐ > ☐ > ☐

Smallest　　　Greatest

☐ < ☐ < ☐

2 Copy and complete to put the lengths in order, from shortest to longest.

Look for the length with the fewest tens first.

a) 30  , 28 and 37

Shortest   Longest

 < <

b) 20  , 70 and 9

Shortest   Longest

 < <

3 a) Find three different numbers that could go in the gap.

CHALLENGE

78 ————————————— 82

b) Which is the smallest number that could go in the gap?

c) Which is the greatest number that could go in the gap?

I will count on from 78.

39

Counting in 2s, 5s and 10s

Discover

1 **a)** There are 20 children already on the .

How many children are there altogether?

b) The arrives at the park.

3 pairs of children get off first.

How many children are still on the ?

40

Share

"I will count them all one by one."

a)

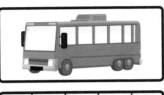 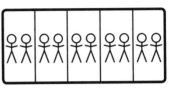

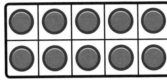 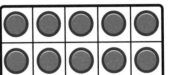

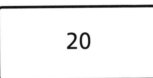 

"I will count on from 20 in twos."

| 20 | 22 | 24 | 26 | 28 | 30 | 32 |

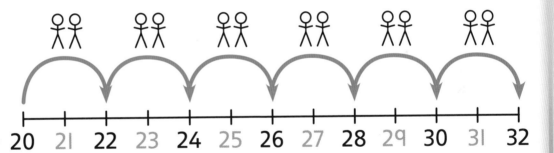

There are 32 children altogether.

b)

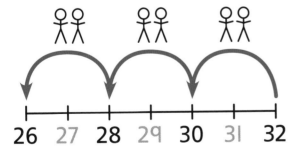

26 children are still on the .

Think together

1 10 children are in the hall.

The rest are in groups of 5 outside.

Copy and complete the number line.

How many children are there altogether?

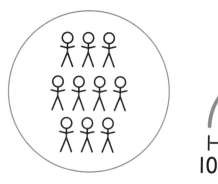

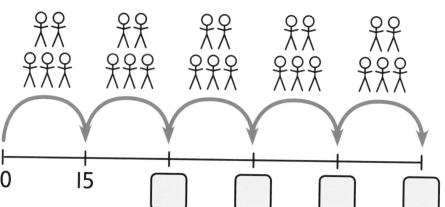

2 Copy and complete these counts.

a)

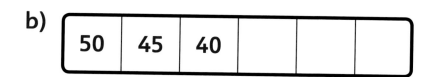

b)

50	45	40			

c) 75, 65, ☐, 45, ☐, ☐

d) 90, 88, ☐, ☐, 82, ☐

3 Copy and complete the number cards.

CHALLENGE

a) 2 less   2 more

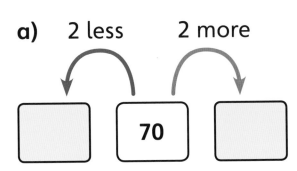

| | 70 | |

c) 5 less   5 more

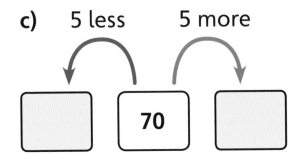

| | 70 | |

b) 2 less   2 more

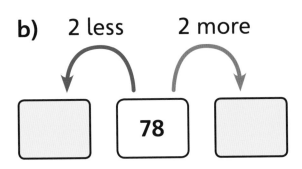

| | 78 | |

d) 10 less   10 more

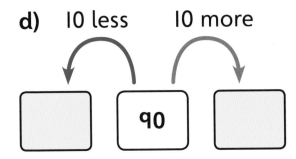

| | 90 | |

I will count in 2s, 5s or 10s to check my answers.

43

→ Practice book 2A p30

Counting in 3s

Discover

I **a)** How many ▱ did Andy use?

b) Andy wants to add another row of △ at the bottom.

How many more ▱ does he need?

Share

I will count the sticks one by one.

I will count in threes.

a)

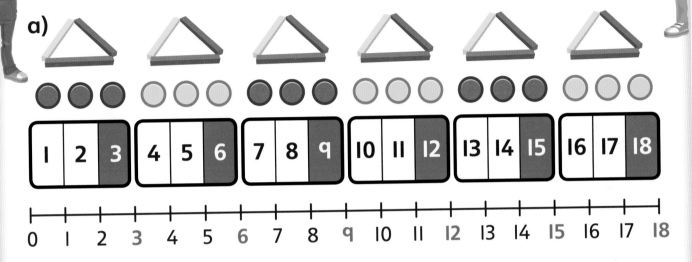

Andy used 18 ⬭.

b) There are 4 triangles in the next row.

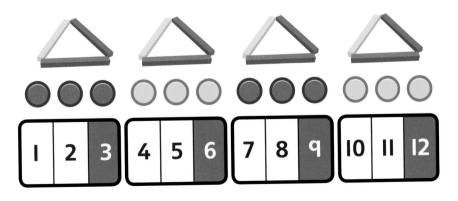

Andy needs 12 more ⬭.

Think together

Count in threes.

1 **a)** How many trees are there?

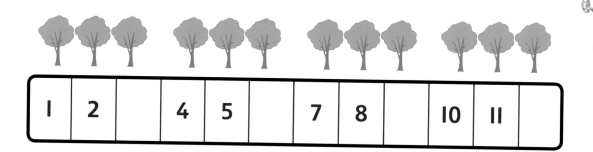

1	2		4	5		7	8		10	11	

b) How many birds are there?

1	2		4	5		7	8		10	11		13	14	

2 **a)** Steve's castle has 12 red ☐.

How many ☐ did Steve use altogether?

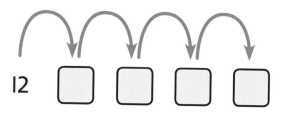

12

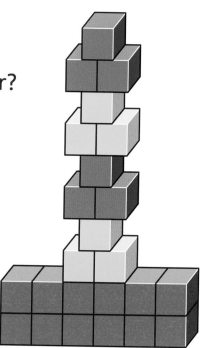

46

b) Olive's castle has 18 red .

How many  did Olive use altogether?

18

3 Jake counts up in 2s from 2.

2	4					

Zara counts up in 3s from 3.

3	6					

Which numbers do Jake and Zara both write?

Are there any other numbers they will both write?

CHALLENGE

47

→ Practice book 2A p33

End of unit check

Your teacher will ask you these questions.

1 How many 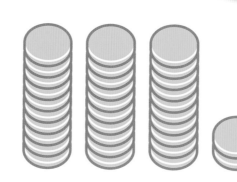 ?

A 23	**B** 32	**C** 5	**D** 50

2 What is shown?

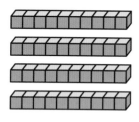

A 4 tens and 5 ones is 45   **C** 4 ones and 4 tens is 44

B 5 tens and 4 ones is 54   **D** 5 ones and 4 tens is 54

3 Which diagram does not represent this number?

4 1

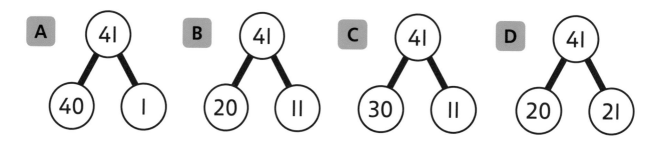

A 41 — 40, 1   **B** 41 — 20, 11   **C** 41 — 30, 11   **D** 41 — 20, 21

4 Which number could not go in the box?

 is greater than 55 but less than 63.

A 59 **B** 60 **C** 53 **D** 62

5 Which number will all the children say?

Mia says 'I am counting in twos: 0, 2, 4…'.

Ben says 'I am counting in fives: 0, 5, 10…'.

Keiko says 'I am counting in threes: 0, 3, 6…'.

A 10 **B** 30 **C** 15 **D** 21

Think!

Which diagram shows a different number?

Prove it.

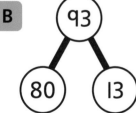

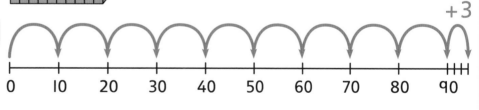

A 9 3

B 93 → 80, 13

C (blocks)

D number line 0 to 90, +3

These words might help you.

tens   ones

part whole   number line

49

→ Practice book 2A p36

Unit 2
Addition and subtraction ①

In this unit we will ...
- ⚡ Use related number facts
- ⚡ Compare number sentences
- ⚡ Make number bonds to 100
- ⚡ Add and subtract ones and tens
- ⚡ Add a 2-digit and a 1-digit number
- ⚡ Subtract a 1-digit number from a 2-digit number

We have used this before. What is the same? What is different?

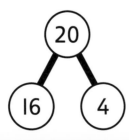

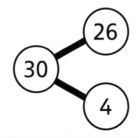

We need some maths words.
Are any of these new?

fact family   **number sentence**

number bonds   **column**

10 more   **10 less**

How many ✏ are there altogether? You can use ▦ and ◯ to find the total.

10

10

Related facts – addition and subtraction

Discover

1 **a)** Copy and complete each ⅄.

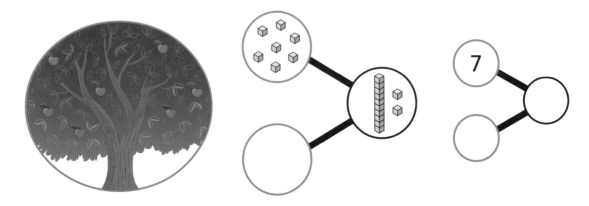

What does each number represent?

b) Copy and complete the **fact family**.

⬜ + ⬜ = ⬜   ⬜ – ⬜ = ⬜

⬜ + ⬜ = ⬜   ⬜ – ⬜ = ⬜

52   What does each number sentence tell you?

Share

a)

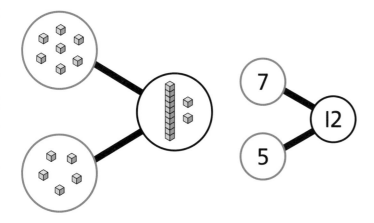

 The number 7 represents in the tree.

The number 5 represents on the ground.

The number 12 represents in total.

b) 7 + 5 = 12

5 + 7 = 12

These number sentences both tell you how many 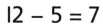 there are altogether.

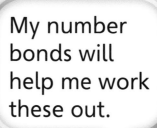 Each number sentence works out something in the picture. Together, they are called a fact family.

12 − 5 = 7

This number sentence tells you how many are in the tree.

12 − 7 = 5

This number sentence tells you how many are on the ground.

My number bonds will help me work these out.

Think together

1. Copy and complete the 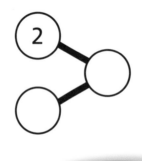 and the number sentences.

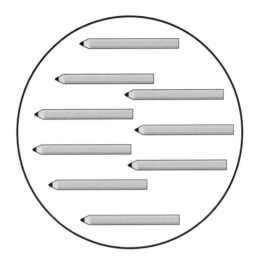

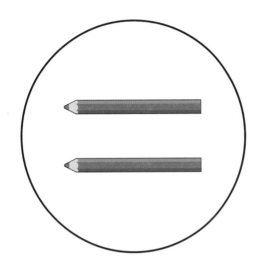

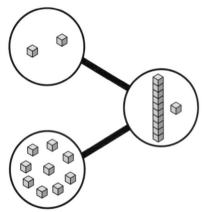

2 + ☐ = ☐

☐ + 2 = ☐

☐ − 2 = ☐

☐ − ☐ = 2

I will count how many pencils of each colour there are.

2 Match each number sentence to what it shows.

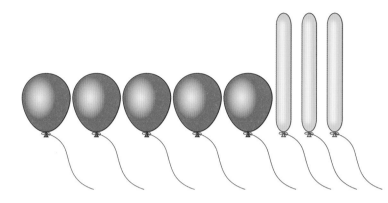

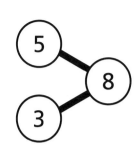

1 5 + 3 = 8

A The number of  .

2 8 − 5 = 3

B The number of ⫰ .

3 8 − 3 = 5

C The number of altogether.

3 Find the number sentences that are shown by this  .

CHALLENGE

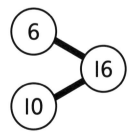

There are 8 to find. Can we find them all?

55

→ Practice book 2A p38

Using number facts to check calculations

Discover

That will be £14, please.

£14

£5   £9

Pet Shop

1 **a)** Check the total cost of the cat bed and the dish by adding the prices together.

b) What other calculations could you do to check your answer?

Share

a)

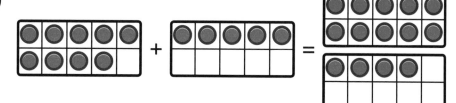

$$9 \quad + \quad 5 \quad = \quad 14$$

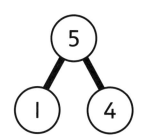

I used 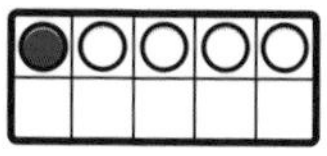  to work out the total cost.

5
6 7 8 9 10 11 12 13 14 15

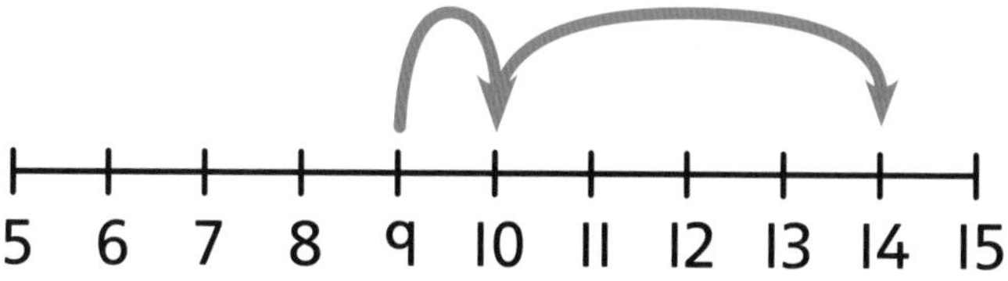

£9 + £5 = £14

The total cost is £14.

I used 1 2 3 4 5 6 7 8 9 10 to work out the total cost.

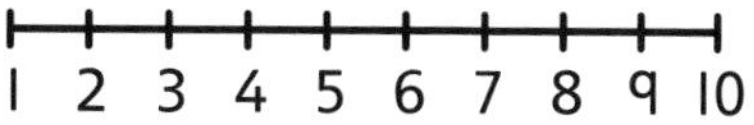

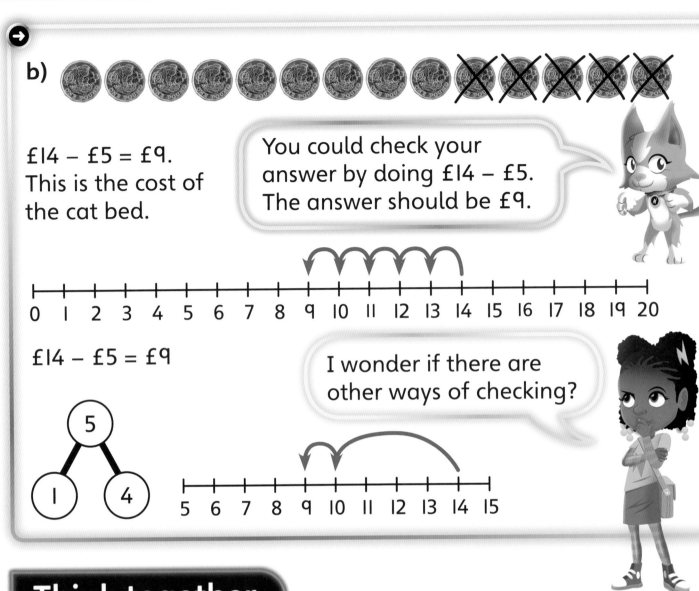

b)

£14 – £5 = £9.
This is the cost of
the cat bed.

You could check your
answer by doing £14 – £5.
The answer should be £9.

£14 – £5 = £9

I wonder if there are
other ways of checking?

Think together

1   Is the total price correct?

What subtraction can
you do to check?

£12

£19

£6

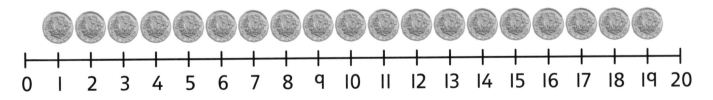

$\boxed{} - \boxed{} = \boxed{}$

2 What addition can you do to check the total price of
the clothes?

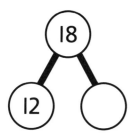

The missing part is 6.

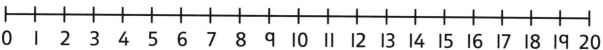

0 1 2 3 4 5 6 7 8 9 10 11 12 13 14 15 16 17 18 19 20

⬚ + ⬚ = ⬚

3 Which of these calculations will help you check
if 5 + 8 = 13 is correct?

CHALLENGE

13 + 5

8 + 5

13 – 5

I think there is a
connection between
these calculations
and the fact families.

8 – 5

13 – 8

Explain why you chose your answers.

I just did 5 + 8 again and
got 13, so it must be right.

59

→ Practice book 2A p41

Comparing number sentences

Discover

1 **a)** Did Ola or Ben bake more cookies?

b) Did Abbie or Ola bake more cookies?

Find the answers without adding up the numbers.

Share

> If I put the cookies in lines, I can see who baked more cookies.

a) Ola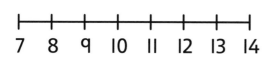

Ben

> I did 7 + 4 = 11 and compared this to 12.

Ola baked 11 cookies. Ben baked 12 cookies.

12 > 11

Ben baked more cookies than Ola.

b) Ola

Abbie

> Each person has one tray with 7 cookies on. I just need to see how many cookies are on the other trays.

7 + 6 > 7 + 4

As 6 is greater than 4 then Abbie baked more cookies than Ola.

Think together

 Tim

 Lin

1 Does Lin or Tim have more flowers?

4 + 8 > ⬜ + ⬜

_____ has more flowers.

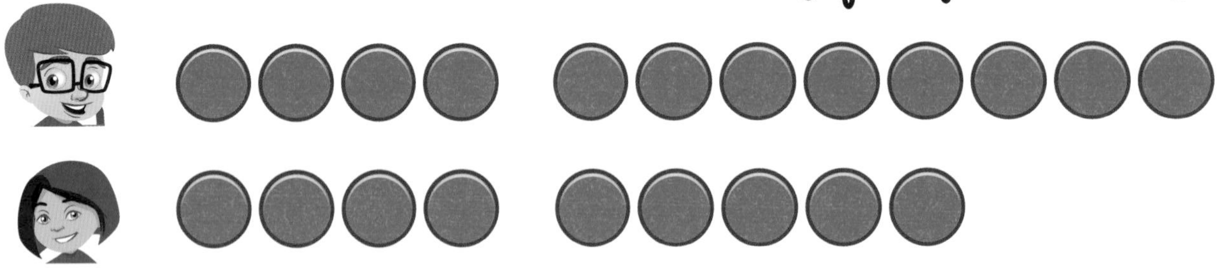

2 Anna and Shaan each had .

I used 2 tissues.

I used 4 tissues.

Anna

Shaan

Does Anna or Shaan have fewer tissues left?

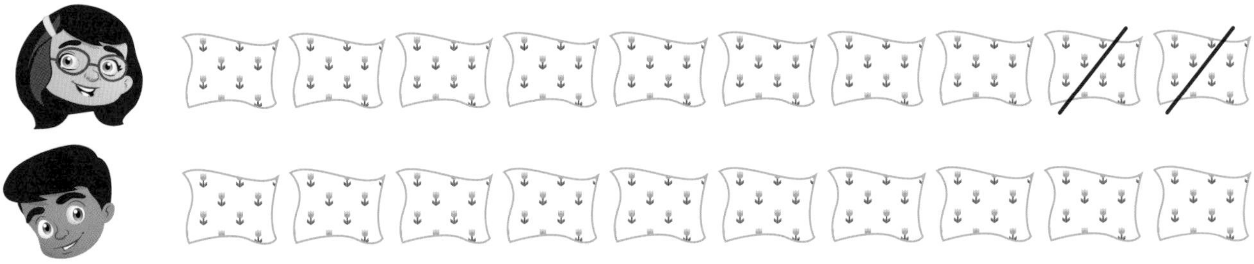

10 − ⬜ ◯ 10 − ⬜

_____ has fewer tissues left.

3 What numbers could go in each box?

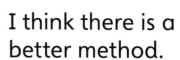

$6 + \boxed{} > 6 + 8$

$10 - 3 < \boxed{} - 3$

What are the smallest whole numbers that work?

I am going to try any numbers.

I think there is a better method.

63

→ Practice book 2A p44

Finding related facts

Discover

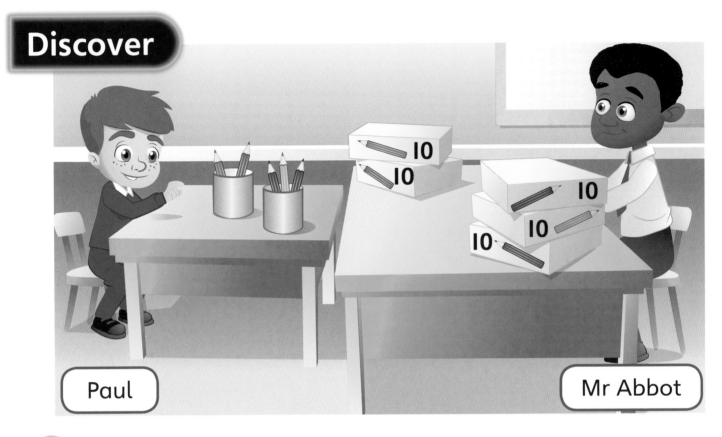

Paul

Mr Abbot

1 **a)** How many pencils does Paul have?

Copy and complete the diagrams to help you fill in the number sentence.

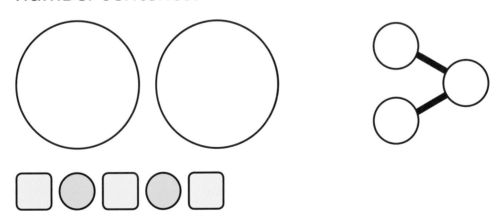

b) How many pencils does Mr Abbot have?

What is the same? What is different?

Share

a)

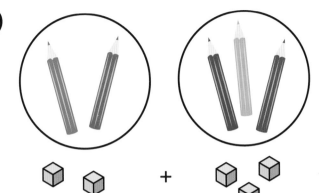

2 + 3 = 5

Paul has 5 pencils.

I wrote 5 = 2 + 3.

b)

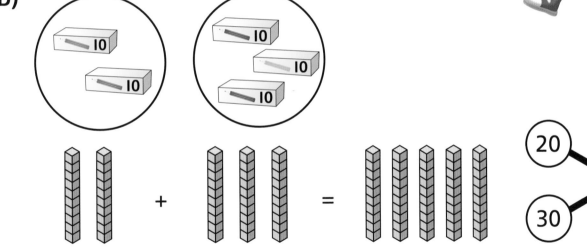

20 + 30 = 50

Mr Abbot has 50 pencils.

The signs and some of the digits are the same.

Some of the numbers are ones. Some of the numbers are tens.

Think together

1 How many pencils are there?

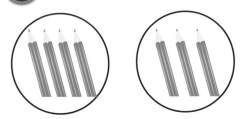

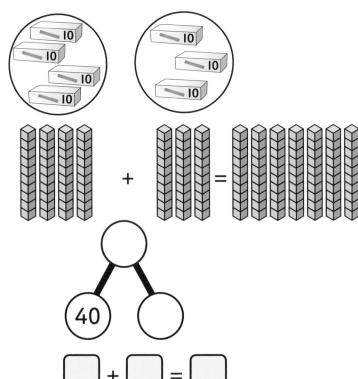

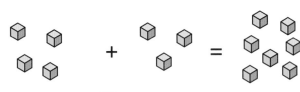

7

4   3

4 + 3 = ▢

40

▢ + ▢ = ▢

There are ▢ pencils.

2 Copy and complete the 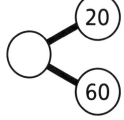 and the number sentences.

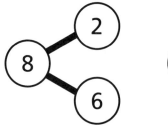

2

8

6

20

60

8 − 6 = ▢

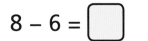

80 − 60 = ▢

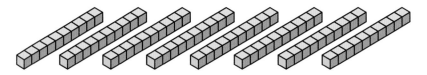

CHALLENGE

3 Here is a number sentence.

$5 + 1 = 6$

Copy and complete the number sentences.

$50 + 10 = \boxed{}$

$60 - \boxed{} = 50$

$10 = \boxed{} - 50$

$50 + 10 = \boxed{} + 50$

I used  to help me get the answers.

I used the number sentence $5 + 1 = 6$ to get the answers.

67

Making number bonds to 100

Discover

1 **a)** How many squares does 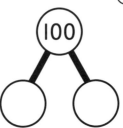 have to move to get to 100?

Complete the number sentence and the ⅄.

87 + ▢ = 100

(100)

b) How many squares does △ have to move to get to 100?

Complete the number sentence and the ⅄.

51 + ▢ = 100

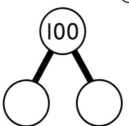

(100)

Share

a)

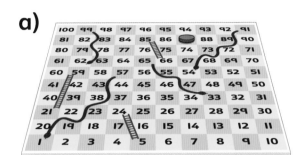

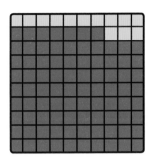

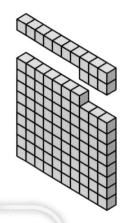

$87 + 13 = 100$

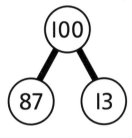

I counted the squares left.

 has to move 13 squares.

b)

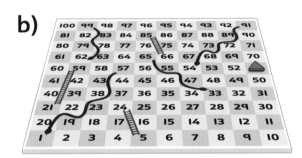

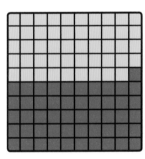

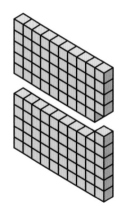

I counted the tens first. Then I counted the ones needed to make 100.

$51 + 49 = 100$

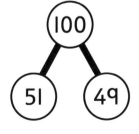

△ has to move 49 squares.

Think together

1 How many more squares does 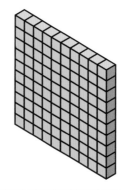 have to move to get to 100?

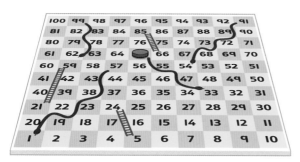 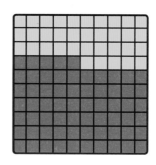 

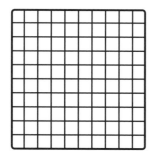 has to move ▢ squares.

$65 + \boxed{} = 100$

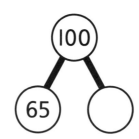

2 What number is missing from the bar model?

100	
	30

$30 + \boxed{} = 100$

3 **a)** Find the missing number.

Copy and complete the .

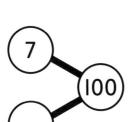 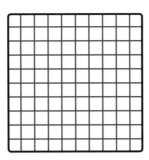 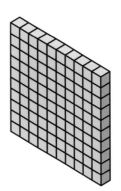

> I used the ▦ and ▨ to help me get the answer.

b) What mistake has been made?

$44 + 66 = 100$

> I know that 4 and 6 make 10. This could help me find the answer.

71

→ Practice book 2A p50

Adding and subtracting 1s

Discover

1 **a)** How many  are there in total?

Write a number sentence to show your answer.

b) Three people each eat one .

How many  are left?

Write a number sentence to show this.

Share

a)

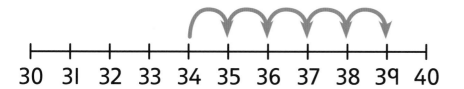

I counted on from 34.

```
30  31  32  33  34  35  36  37  38  39  40
```

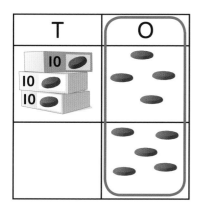
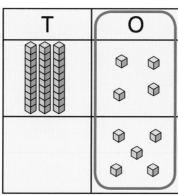

T	O
3	4
+	5
	q

I ordered my work in columns. First, I added the ones.

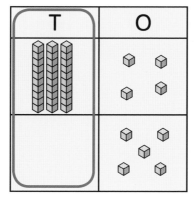

T	O
3	4
+	5
3	q

Then I added the tens.

$34 + 5 = 39$

There are 39 in total.

73

b)

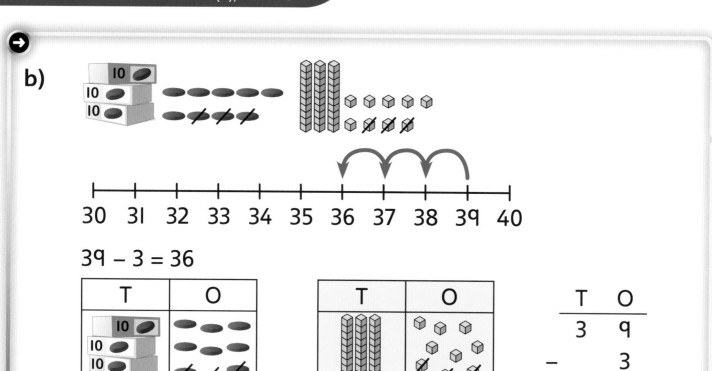

$39 - 3 = 36$

T	O

T	O

```
  T  O
  3  9
-    3
-----
  3  6
```

There are 36 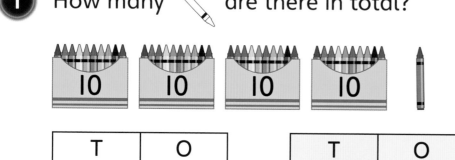 left.

Think together

I How many ✏ are there in total?

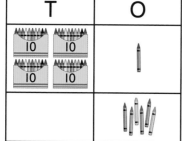

T	O

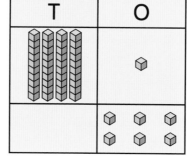

T	O

```
    T  O
    4  1
+      6
-------
```

$41 + 6 = \boxed{}$ There are $\boxed{}$ ✏ in total.

2 There are 26 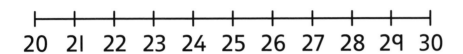.

Five people each eat 1 ⊙.

How many ⊙ are left?

```
├──┼──┼──┼──┼──┼──┼──┼──┼──┼──┤
20  21  22  23  24  25  26  27  28  29  30
```

 – ☐ = ☐

There are ☐ ⊙ left.

3 Callie and Romesh are working out calculations.

Are their workings correct?

a) 42 + 5

Callie

T	O
4	2
+	5
4	7

Romesh

T	O
4	2
+ 5	
9	2

b) 65 – 3

Romesh

T	O
6	5
–	3
6	2

Callie

T	O
	3
– 6	5
6	2

75

→ Practice book 2A p53

Finding 10 more and 10 less

Discover

1 a) The ⬤ player gets **10 more** points.

How many points does ⬤ player have now?

b) The ◯ player loses 10 points.

How many points does ◯ player have now?

Share

a) player has 40 points.

 player wins 10 more points.

1	2	3	4	5	6	7	8	9	10
11	12	13	14	15	16	17	18	19	20
21	22	23	24	25	26	27	28	29	30
31	32	33	34	35	36	37	38	39	40
41	42	43	44	45	46	47	48	49	50
51	52	53	54	55	56	57	58	59	60
61	62	63	64	65	66	67	68	69	70
71	72	73	74	75	76	77	78	79	80
81	82	83	84	85	86	87	88	89	90
91	92	93	94	95	96	97	98	99	100

> I tried to find a pattern on a ▦ .
> First, I found 40.
>
> 10 more than 40 is 50.
> This is one more row on the ▦ .

1	2	3	4	5	6	7	8	9	10
11	12	13	14	15	16	17	18	19	20
21	22	23	24	25	26	27	28	29	30
31	32	33	34	35	36	37	38	39	40
41	42	43	44	45	46	47	48	49	50
51	52	53	54	55	56	57	58	59	60
61	62	63	64	65	66	67	68	69	70
71	72	73	74	75	76	77	78	79	80
81	82	83	84	85	86	87	88	89	90
91	92	93	94	95	96	97	98	99	100

10 more

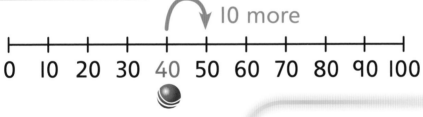

0 10 20 30 40 50 60 70 80 90 100

> I showed 10 more on a number line.
> 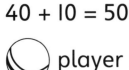 player had 40 points so I started at 40.

10 more than 40 is 50.

$40 + 10 = 50$

 player now has 50 points.

b)

1	2	3	4	5	6	7	8	9	10
11	12	13	14	15	16	17	18	19	20
21	22	23	24	25	26	27	28	29	30
31	32	33	34	35	36	37	38	39	40
41	42	43	44	45	46	47	48	49	50
51	52	53	54	55	56	57	58	59	60
61	62	63	64	65	66	67	68	69	70
71	72	73	74	75	76	77	78	79	80
81	82	83	84	85	86	87	88	89	90
91	92	93	94	95	96	97	98	99	100

10 less than 57 is 47.

$57 - 10 = 47$

◯ player now has 47 points.

I showed 10 fewer on a ▦.

Think together

 76  WIN 10 LOSE 10

1 How many points does ◯ player have?

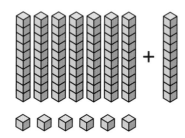

1	2	3	4	5	6	7	8	9	10
11	12	13	14	15	16	17	18	19	20
21	22	23	24	25	26	27	28	29	30
31	32	33	34	35	36	37	38	39	40
41	42	43	44	45	46	47	48	49	50
51	52	53	54	55	56	57	58	59	60
61	62	63	64	65	66	67	68	69	70
71	72	73	74	75	76	77	78	79	80
81	82	83	84	85	86	87	88	89	90
91	92	93	94	95	96	97	98	99	100

10 more than 76 is ☐.

$76 + 10 = ☐$

◯ player has ☐ points.

2

1	2	3	4	5	6	7	8	9	10
11	12	13	14	15	16	17	18	19	20
21	22	23	24	25	26	27	28	29	30
31	32	33	34	35	36	37	38	39	40
41	42	43	44	45	46	47	48	49	50
51	52	53	54	55	56	57	58	59	60
61	62	63	64	65	66	67	68	69	70
71	72	73	74	75	76	77	78	79	80
81	82	83	84	85	86	87	88	89	90
91	92	93	94	95	96	97	98	99	100

a) Copy and complete the number track.

20	30							

b) Copy and complete the number track.

84	74				34			

3 Copy these sentences and answer the questions.

CHALLENGE

10 more than 73 is ☐.

35 is 10 more than ☐.

10 less than 99 is ☐.

60 is 10 less than ☐.

1	2	3	4	5	6	7	8	9	10
11	12	13	14	15	16	17	18	19	20
21	22	23	24	25	26	27	28	29	30
31	32	33	34	35	36	37	38	39	40
41	42	43	44	45	46	47	48	49	50
51	52	53	54	55	56	57	58	59	60
61	62	63	64	65	66	67	68	69	70
71	72	73	74	75	76	77	78	79	80
81	82	83	84	85	86	87	88	89	90
91	92	93	94	95	96	97	98	99	100

On a ▦ , is 10 more than a number on the line above or below?

On a ▦ , is 10 less than a number on the line above or below?

79

→ **Practice book 2A p56**

Adding and subtracting 10s

Discover

I **a)** How many  are there in total?

b) There are 65 people at the fireworks.

40 of the people are adults.

How many of the people are children?

Share

First, I added the ones. I remembered that 30 is 3 tens and 0 ones.

a)

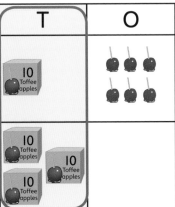

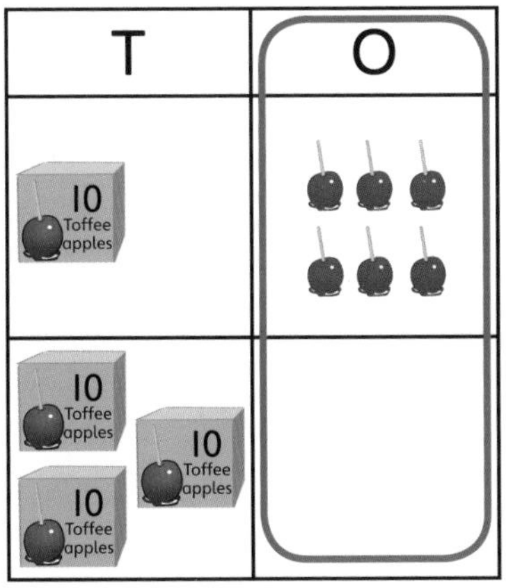

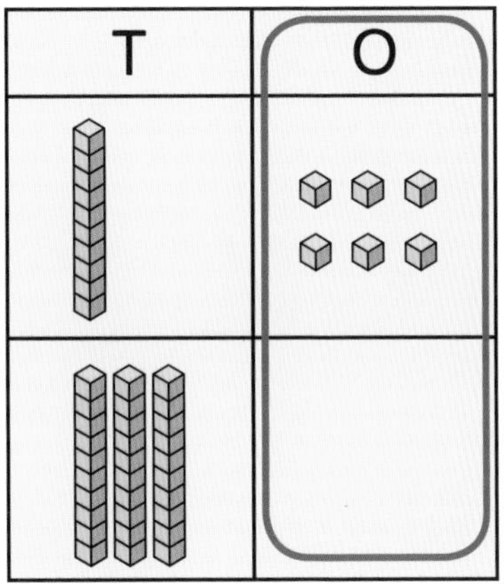

T	O
1	6
+ 3	0
	6

Next, I added the tens.

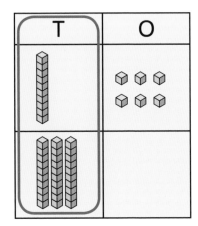

T	O
1	6
+ 3	0
4	6

16 + 30 = 46

There are 46 🍎 in total.

b)

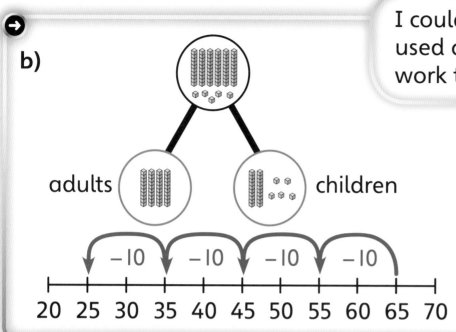

I could have used columns to work this out.

There are 25 children at the fireworks.

Think together

1 How many 🎆 are there in total?

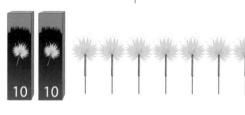
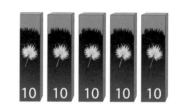

	T	O

	T	O

```
    T   O
    2   7
+   5   0
  _____
```

27 + 50 = ☐

There are ☐ 🎆 in total.

I could have used a number line to work this out.

2 A tray contains 10 pieces of toffee.

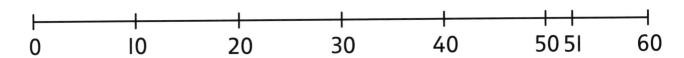

40 pieces of toffee are sold.

How many pieces of toffee are left?

51 − 40 = ☐

There are ☐ pieces of toffee left.

3 Find the mistakes in the calculations.

What is the correct answer?

CHALLENGE

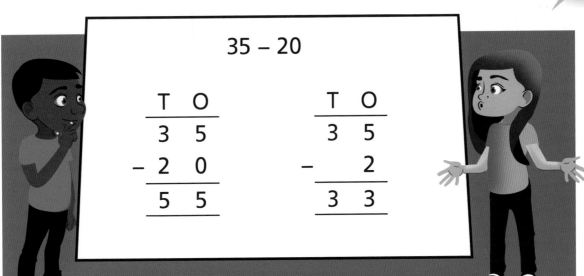

$$35 - 20$$

T	O
3	5
− 2	0
5	5

T	O
3	5
−	2
3	3

83

→ **Practice book 2A p59**

Adding a 2-digit number and a 1-digit number ❶

Discover

❶ **a)** Use ◯ and ⊞⊞⊞⊞ to show the chairs that are stacked.

How many stacked chairs are there?

b) How many chairs are there in total?

Share

a)

There are 45 stacked chairs.

b)

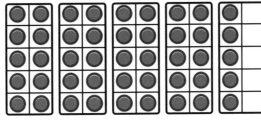

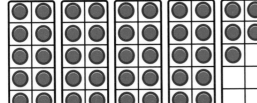  +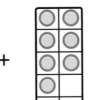

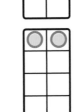 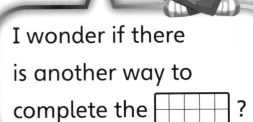

I wonder if there is another way to complete the ☐☐☐☐☐ ?

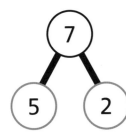

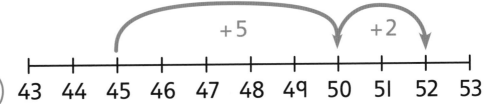

43 44 45 46 47 48 49 50 51 52 53

+5   +2

There are 52 chairs in total.

45 + 7 = 45 + 5 + 2 = 52

First, I added on 5 to make 50. If the whole is 7 and one of the parts is 5, then the other part is 2. So next, I added on 2.

85

Think together

1 How many are there in total?

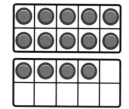 + 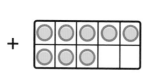 =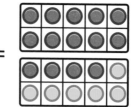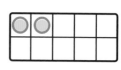

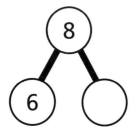

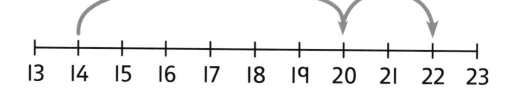

13 14 15 16 17 18 19 20 21 22 23

$14 + 8 = 14 + \boxed{} + \boxed{} = \boxed{}$

There are $\boxed{}$ in total.

2 How many ⭐ are there in total?

$27 + 8 = 27 + \boxed{} + \boxed{} = \boxed{}$

There are $\boxed{}$ ⭐ in total.

3 Copy and complete each number sentence.

a) $42 + 9 = 42 + \boxed{} + \boxed{} = \boxed{}$

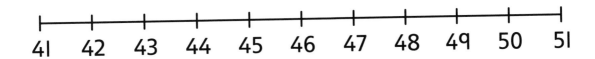

I also used $\bigcirc$ and ▦ to help me.

b) $48 + \boxed{} = 48 + \boxed{} + 5 = 55$

c) $2\boxed{} + 7 = 2\boxed{} + 1 + \boxed{} = \boxed{}$

I wonder how many methods I could use to work out 8 + 43.

87

→ **Practice book 2A p62**

Adding a 2-digit number and a 1-digit number ❷

Discover

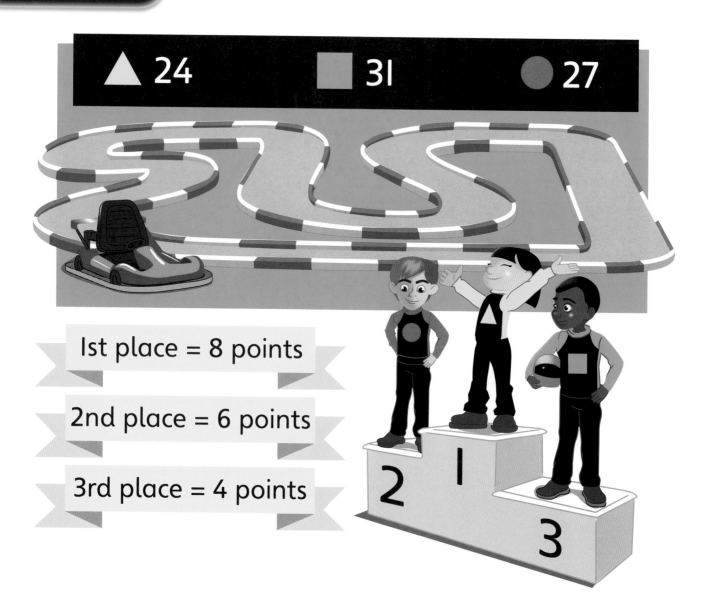

▲ 24   ■ 31   ● 27

1st place = 8 points

2nd place = 6 points

3rd place = 4 points

1 **a)** How many points does △ team now have?

b) Which team scored most points?

Share

a) 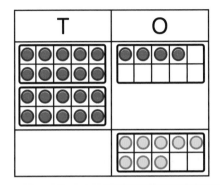 team came first so they received 8 points. They already had 24 points.

I added the ones first. I could exchange 12 ones for 1 ten and 2 ones. Next, I added the tens.

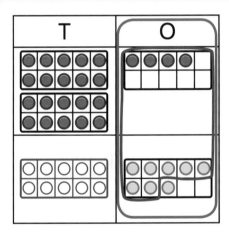

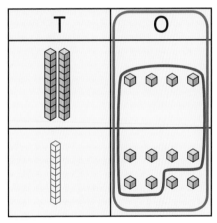

I could have used a number line to help me.

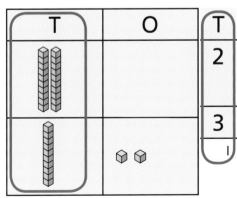

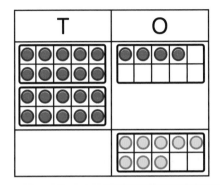 team now has 32 points.

b) ☐ team   ○ team

T	O

```
  T  O
  3  1
+    4
-------
     5
```

T	O

```
  T  O
  2  7
+    6
-------
     3
  1
```

☐ team scored most points.

Think together

① How many  are there in total?

  +

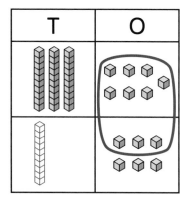

```
  T  O
  3  7
+    6
-------
  ☐
  ☐
```

First, I added the ones. I circled 10 ⬡ to make 1 ▭.

There are ☐ 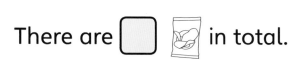 in total.

90

2 Use a different method to find each missing number.

a)

?	
48	8

b)

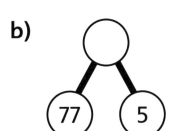

You now know two methods. Which method did you like best?

3 Four children used four different methods to work out 52 + 9. Explain each method to your partner.

CHALLENGE

```
  T  O
  5  2
+    9
-------
  6  1     I used
     1     columns.
```

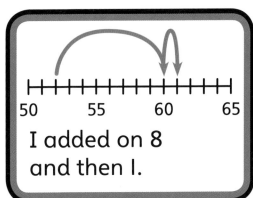

50   55   60   65

I added on 8 and then 1.

I added on 10 and subtracted 1.

I know my bonds within 20. I know that 2 + 9 = 11. So 52 + 9 = 61.

→ Practice book 2A p65

Subtracting a 1-digit number from a 2-digit number ❶

Discover

Class 2: 35 children

Not in today:

Amira

Hanan

Emma

James

Ali

Bob

Total:

❶ **a)** Represent the 35 children in Class 2 using

⬤◯◯◯◯ and ▭▭▭▭▭▭▭▭▭▭ .

b) Today 6 children are away.

How many children are in Class 2 today?

☐ – ☐ = ☐

Share

a) Children in Class 2.

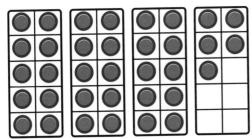

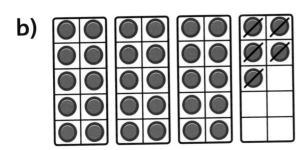

b)

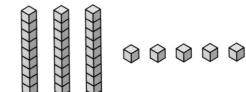

We can do the subtraction in two parts. We subtract 5 first.

35 – 5 = 30

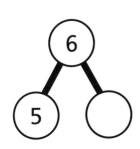

I know that if the whole is 6 and one of the parts is 5, then the other part is 1. So I will subtract 1 more.

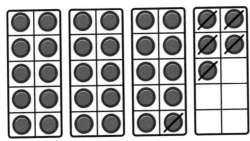

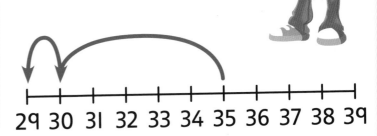

29 30 31 32 33 34 35 36 37 38 39

30 – 1 = 29

35 – 5 – 1 = 29

There are 29 children in Class 2 today.

93

Think together

1

24 children have their hand up.

6 of the children put their hand down.

How many children still have their hand up?

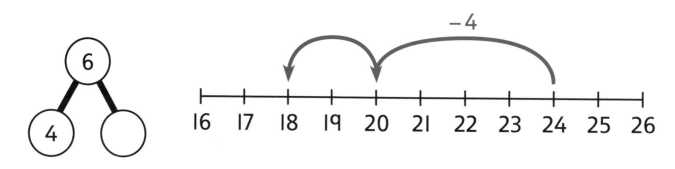

$24 - 6 = 24 - 4 - \boxed{} = \boxed{}$

There are $\boxed{}$ children with their hand still up.

2 What is 73 – 5?

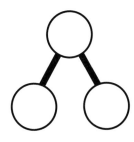

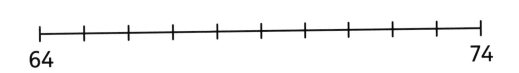

64   74

73 – ☐ – ☐ = ☐

73 – 5 = ☐

3 Copy and complete these number sentences.

CHALLENGE

a) 34 – 7 = 34 – 4 – ☐ = ☐

b) 46 – 7 = 46 – ☐ – 1 = ☐

c) 55 – 7 = 55 – ☐ – ☐ = ☐

d) 4☐ – 7 = 4☐ – 1 – 6 = ☐

Use a number line to help you.

95

Subtracting a 1-digit number from a 2-digit number ②

Discover

1 **a)** Amy puts 1  in each cup.

How many will Amy have left?

b) Amy gives some of the she has left to her friend Liam.

Now she has 9 left.

How many did Amy give to Liam?

96

Share

a)

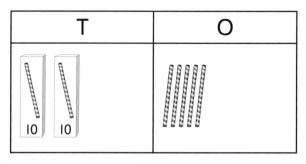

T	O

	T	O

$$\begin{array}{r} T\ O \\ 2\ 5 \\ -\quad\ 7 \\ \hline \end{array}$$

I looked at the ones column first. I exchanged 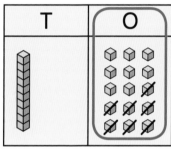 for so I could subtract 7.

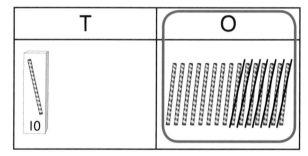

T	O

	T	O

$$\begin{array}{r} T\ O \\ {}^1\!\not2\ {}^1\!5 \\ -\quad\ 7 \\ \hline \quad\ 8 \end{array}$$

Next, I subtracted the tens. I ten subtract 0 tens is I ten.

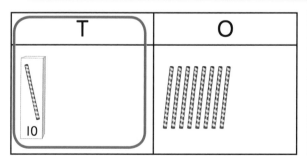

T	O

	T	O

$$\begin{array}{r} T\ O \\ {}^1\!\not2\ {}^1\!5 \\ -\quad\ 7 \\ \hline 1\ \ 8 \end{array}$$

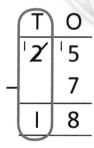

25 – 7 = 18

Amy has 18 straws left.

b)

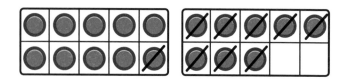

$18 - 9 = 9$

Amy gave 9 straws to Liam.

Think together

1 Mai has some bread rolls. She sells 8 of them.

How many bread rolls are left?

T	O
(4 tens)	(3 ones)

```
  T   O
  4   3
-     8
─────────
```

T	O
(3 tens)	(5 ones)

```
   T    O
  ³4   ¹3
-       8
─────────
  [ ] [ ]
```

There are ☐ bread rolls left.

2 Work out the missing number.

65 – 9 = ☐

3 What is the same in these calculations?

What is different?

```
  T  O          T  O
  3  7          3  4
-    4        -    7
```

These calculations have the same digits in.
I think they answer the same question.

I am not sure. I think they give different answers.
I wonder why the answers are different?

99

→ Practice book 2A p71

End of unit check

Your teacher
will ask you
these questions.

1 Which two numbers do not add up to make 100?

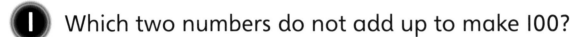

A 24 and 76   **B**   **C**   **D** 10 and 90

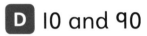

Use the number square to help you.

1	2	3	4	5	6	7	8	9	10
11	12	13	14	15	16	17	18	19	20
21	22	23	24	25	26	27	28	29	30
31	32	33	34	35	36	37	38	39	40
41	42	43	44	45	46	47	48	49	50
51	52	53	54	55	56	57	58	59	60
61	62	63	64	65	66	67	68	69	70
71	72	73	74	75	76	77	78	79	80
81	82	83	84	85	86	87	88	89	90
91	92	93	94	95	96	97	98	99	100

2 What number should go in the shaded box?

23	33	43	53				

A 93   **B** 56   **C** 73   **D** 83

3 Which calculation gives a different answer to the others?

A 43 + 5 **B** 42 + 6 **C** 38 + 10 **D** 18 + 20

4 A box contains 64 pencils.

There are 8 yellow pencils. The rest are green.

Which calculation shows how many green pencils?

A 64 − 8 **C** 64 − 4 − 5

B 64 + 8 **D** 8 − 64

5 What is the difference between 35 and 9?

A 26 **B** 27 **C** 34 **D** 45

Think!

Miss Jamil says, 'What is 56 + 20?'
Freya says, '58.'
Jack says, '36.'
Mira says, '56 + 10 is 76 and + 10 is 86.'

What mistake has each child made?

These words
might help you.

tens   ones   add

total   subtract

101

→ Practice book 2A p74

Unit 3
Addition and subtraction ②

In this unit we will …
- ⚡ Add two 2-digit numbers
- ⚡ Subtract 2-digit numbers
- ⚡ Add three 1-digit numbers
- ⚡ Solve word problems

How many more red 🌼

are there than yellow 🌼 ?

Use this to find out.

We will need some maths words. Do you remember them?

total   tens   ones

subtract   difference

bar model   represent

This will help! Use it to find the total of 16 + 7.

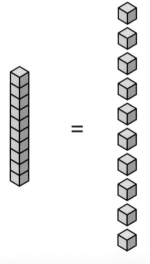

Adding two 2-digit numbers 1

Discover

1   a) What is the total score for the team wearing red checks?

b) The plain green team scores 10 more than the red checks.

Where does the other plain green ◁ land?

Share

a)

Tens	Ones
‖‖‖	▫ ▫
‖	▫ ▫ ▫ ▫

+

```
  T  O
  3  2
+ 1  4
_____
```

Tens	Ones
‖‖‖	▫ ▫
‖	▫ ▫ ▫ ▫

+

```
  T │ O
  3 │ 2
+ 1 │ 4
    │ 6
```

I added the ones first and then added the tens.

Tens	Ones
‖‖‖	▫ ▫
‖	▫ ▫ ▫ ▫

+

```
  T │ O
  3 │ 2
+ 1 │ 4
  4 │ 6
```

I started with 32, added 10 and then added 4.

32 + 14 = 46

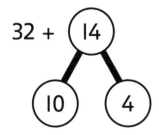

32 + 10 = 42

42 + 4 = 46

The red checks score 46 points in total.

b) 14 + 42 = 56

The other plain green 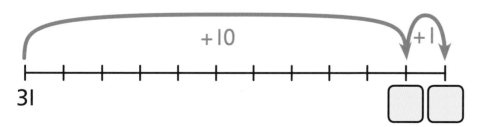 lands on 42.

Think together

1 The blue striped team throw one ☐ on 23 and one on 50.

What total score does the blue striped team get?

Tens	Ones
(4 tens)	
+ (2 tens)	⬦ ⬦ ⬦

```
  T O
  5 0
+ 2 3
_____
```

50 + 23 = ☐

The total score is ☐.

2 Two ☐ are thrown. One lands on 31 and one on 11.

What score does this make?

+10   +1

31 ────────────────────── ☐☐

31 + 10 = ☐

☐ + ☐ = ☐

The total score is ☐.

106

3 One lands on 32 and the other lands on 11.

What score does their team get?

CHALLENGE

Tens	Ones
+	

```
  T O
  3 2
+ 1 1
─────
```

$32 + 11 = \boxed{}$

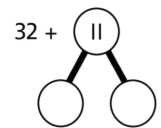
32 +

$32 + \boxed{} = \boxed{}$

$\boxed{} + \boxed{} = \boxed{}$

The total score is $\boxed{}$.

I drew a ▭▭▭▭ to represent ten.
I drew a ⬡ to represent one.

I think I could use the answer to Question 2 for help.

→ **Practice book 2A p76**

Adding two 2-digit numbers ❷

1 **a)** How many points did Asha score in total?

b) Sol throws one more ⭕.

He scores 50 in total.

Where does his other ⭕ land?

Share

a)

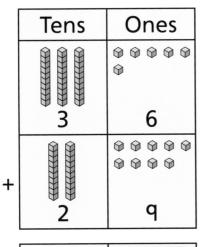

$$\begin{array}{r} \text{T}\quad\text{O} \\ 3\quad6 \\ +\ 2\quad9 \\ \hline \end{array}$$

> I know that 6 ones and 9 ones is 15 ones. I can exchange 10 ones for one ten. So 15 ones is the same as 1 ten and 5 ones.

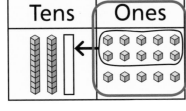

$$\begin{array}{r} \text{T}\quad\text{O} \\ 3\quad6 \\ +\ 2\quad9 \\ \hline 5 \\ {\scriptstyle 1} \end{array}$$

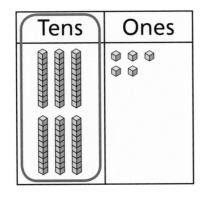

$$\begin{array}{r} \text{T}\quad\text{O} \\ 3\quad6 \\ +\ 2\quad9 \\ \hline 6\quad5 \\ {\scriptstyle 1} \end{array}$$

Asha scored 65 points in total.

> You could also use a number line to do this.

b)

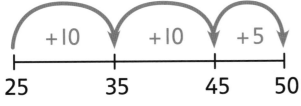

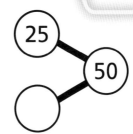

Sol's other lands on 25.

Think together

1 Asha now scores 36 and Sol scores 25.

What is the total score?

Tens	Ones

The total score is ☐.

	T	O
	3	6
+	2	5

2 One ⬭ lands on 17 and one lands on 25.

What is the total score?

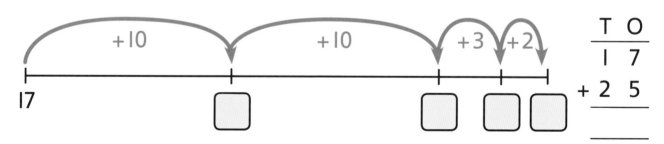

	T	O
	1	7
+	2	5

17 + 20 = ☐

☐ + 3 = ☐

☐ + 2 = ☐

The total score is ☐.

3 One ⬭ lands on 17 and one lands on 29.

What is the total score?

Tens	Ones
▮	◻ ◻ ◻ ◻ ◻ ◻ ◻

+

```
  T O
  1 7
+ 2 9
-----
```

$17 + 29 = \boxed{}$

The total score is $\boxed{}$.

I will use a number line. I will start counting from 29.

Can I use 17 + 25 to help solve 17 + 29?

111

Subtracting a 2-digit number from another 2-digit number ❶

Discover

❶ a) How many eggs are left after Omar bakes a cake?

b) Omar breaks 20 eggs.

How many eggs are left now?

Share

> I will start with the greatest number.

a)

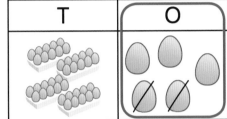

```
 T  O
 4  5
-1  2
```

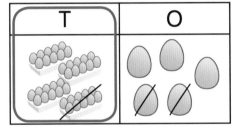

```
 T │ O
 4 │ 5
-1 │ 2
   │ 3
```

> I could try crossing out 12 eggs: 1  and 2 🥚.

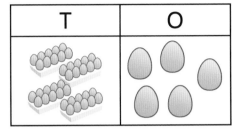

```
 T │ O
 4 │ 5
-1 │ 2
 3 │ 3
```

45 − 12 = 33

There are 33 eggs left.

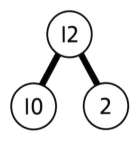

12 = 10 and 2

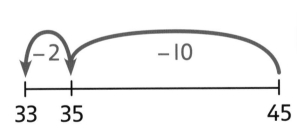

−2   −10
33 35   45

> I used a number line.

b)

Tens	Ones		Tens	Ones

```
 T  O
 3  3
-2  0
 1  3
```

There are 13 eggs left.

113

Think together

1 There are 38 eggs. Harry uses 16 eggs.

How many eggs are left?

T	O

T	O

```
  T  O
  3  8
- 1  6
 [  ][  ]
```

38 ⬭ – 16 🥚 = ☐

2 Eva has 64 eggs. She uses 41 eggs.

How many eggs does she have left?

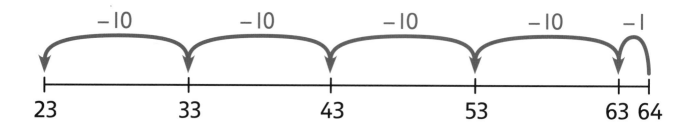

64 – 41 = ☐

Eva has ☐ eggs left.

3 Alfie has 74 eggs. He gives 41 eggs to Rosie.

How many are left?

T	O

```
    T   O
   [ ] [ ]
 - [ ] [ ]
   _____
   [ ] [ ]
```

74 – 41 = ☐

Do we always start with ones for subtraction?

Should we use the same method for subtraction, or change it?

115

Subtracting a 2-digit number from another 2-digit number ❷

Discover

1 **a)** How many points is the 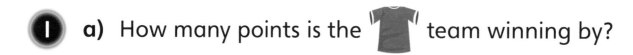 team winning by?

b) The team does not score again and wins

by 15 points.

How many points will the team have at the end?

Share

I subtracted tens first, so the ones stayed the same.

I worked out the numbers in the jumps.

a)

 21 21   26   36   46   **46**

$$- 5 \qquad - 10 \qquad - 10$$

46 – 21 = 25

25 is the **difference** between 46 and 21.

The team in plain red shirts is winning by 25 points.

You could count on instead of counting back.

b) 46 – ☐ = 15

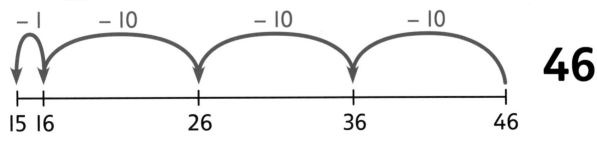

$$- 1 \qquad - 10 \qquad - 10 \qquad - 10$$

15 16   26   36   46

46

46 – 31 = 15

The team in striped blue shirts will have 31 points.

117

Think together

1 How many more points does 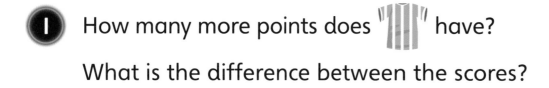 have?

What is the difference between the scores?

22
56

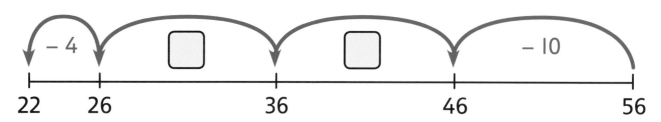

$56 - 22 = \boxed{}$

$\boxed{}$ is the difference between the scores.

2 What is the difference between the scores?

74
31

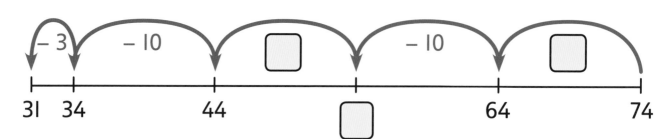

$74 - 31 = \boxed{}$

The difference between the scores is $\boxed{}$.

3 What is the difference between the scores?

Here are 3 ways.

65

31

CHALLENGE

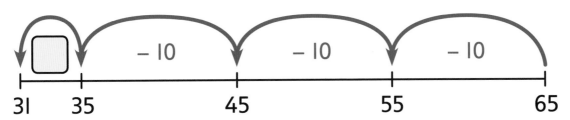

31 35   45   55   65

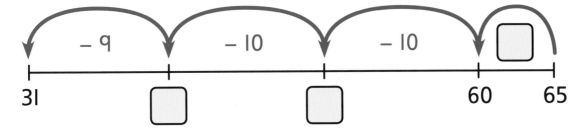

31   60   65

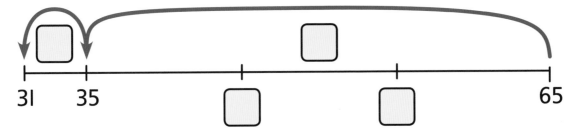

31 35   65

The difference between the scores is ☐.

What is the same?
What is different?

Can you find a different set of jumps to find the difference? And another?

→ Practice book 2A p85

Subtracting a 2-digit number from another 2-digit number ❸

Discover

Strawberry jam: 52 strawberries

① a) Kara has 24 🍓 .

She needs 52 to make jam.

How many more does she need to pick?

b) Ben needs 16 more 🍓 to make jam.

How many 🍓 does he have?

Share

I used a number line to count back, because I need to find the difference.

a) 52 − 24

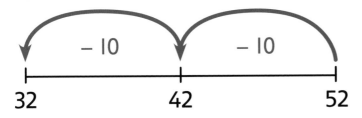

52 − 20 = 32

We know that 4 is made up of 2 and 2. This will help us.

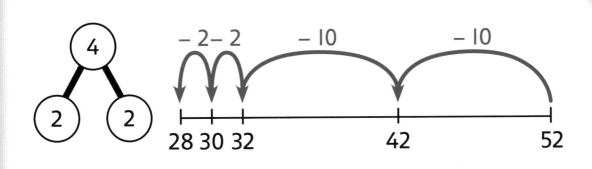

32 − 2 = 30

30 − 2 = 28

Kara needs 28 more to make jam.

b) Ben needs 16 more to make the jam.

He needs 52 in total.

I will count back 16 from 52.

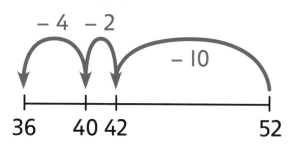

$$52 - 16 = 36$$

Ben has 36 .

Think together

1 Zeb has 71 .

He uses 52 to make some jam.

How many does he have left?

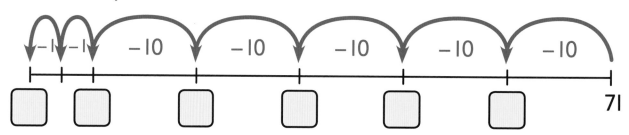

$$71 - 52 = \boxed{}$$

Zeb has $\boxed{}$ left over.

2 Lan has 35  .

She eats 18.

How many does she have left?

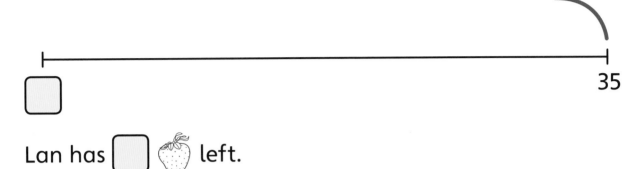

35

Lan has ▢ 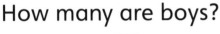 left.

3 There are 64 children picking  . 17 are girls.

How many are boys?

There are ▢ boys.

CHALLENGE

I can do this in different ways. These methods are all subtracting!

Which method do you prefer?

123

Subtracting a 2-digit number from another 2-digit number ❹

Discover

Swimming competition.
First to 45 lengths wins.

Susie: 15 lengths   Charlie: 19 lengths   Kay: 27 lengths

Susie

Charlie

Kay

1 **a)** How many lengths does Susie have left?

b) How many lengths does Kay have left?

Share

a)

Tens	Ones

```
  T   O
  4   5
- 1   5
  3   0
```

Susie has 30 lengths left.

> Subtract the ones first, then the tens. If there are no ones left, I need to use a zero.

b)

Tens	Ones

```
  T   O
  4   5
- 2   7
```

Tens	Ones

```
  T    O
  ³4̶  ¹5
- 2    7
```

> Remember, one ten is equal to ten ones.

Tens	Ones

```
  T    O
  ³4̶  ¹5
- 2    7
       8
```

Tens	Ones

```
  T    O
  ³4̶  ¹5
- 2    7
  1    8
```

45 − 27 = 18   Kay has 18 lengths left.

Think together

 Adults swim 64 lengths in a race.

Mr Peters has swum 47 lengths.

How many does he have left to swim?

Tens	Ones

Tens	Ones

```
  T   O
  6   4
- 4   7
_____
```

Mr Peters has ⬜ more lengths to swim.

2 Miss Stone has to swim 64 lengths.

She has 38 lengths left.

How many lengths has Miss Stone swum?

Tens	Ones

```
  T   O
  6   4
- 3   8
_____
```

Miss Stone has swum ⬜ lengths.

3 Layla swims 43 lengths. Oz swims 18 lengths.

How many more lengths does Layla swim?

Tens	Ones
▮▮▮▮	◇ ◇ ◇

T   O

└─┐ ┌─┐
│ │ │ │
└─┘ └─┘

– ┌─┐ ┌─┐
  │ │ │ │
  └─┘ └─┘
  ┌─┐ ┌─┐
  │ │ │ │
  └─┘ └─┘

├────────────────────────────────────┤
18   43

Layla swims ☐ more lengths than Oz.

I think I can answer this using 2 methods.

I can still see this as a subtraction as I am finding the difference.

127

→ Practice book 2A p91

Adding three 1-digit numbers

Discover

Kendi

Lily

Malik

Target number

1 **a)** How many fingers are being held up altogether to make the target number?

Target number
15

b) How many fingers should Malik show?

Share

I can do 7 + 3 = 10 and then do 10 + 5.

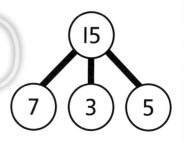

7 + 3 + 5 = 15

a)

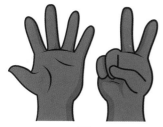    

7   +   3   +   5   = 15

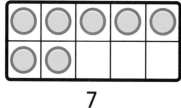 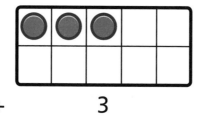 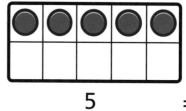

7   +   3   +   5   = 15

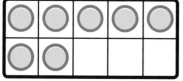  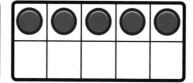

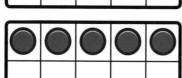

7 + 3 + 5 = 15

I found a number bond to 10. This made it easier to add.

15 fingers are being held up altogether to make the target number.

b)

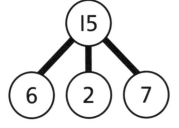

$6 + 2 + 7 = 15$

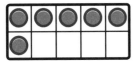 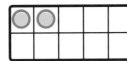 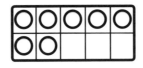 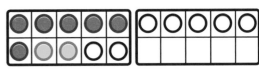

6   +   2   +   7   =   15

Malik should show 7 fingers.

Think together

1 How many fingers are there?

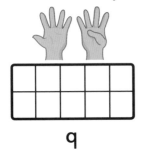   +   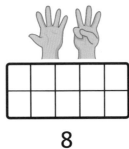   +   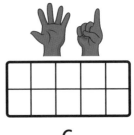   =   ☐

q   +   8   +   6

There are ☐ fingers in total.

2 What is the missing number?

Target number
19

$= 8 + 5 +$ ☐

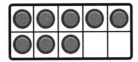   +   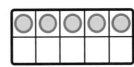   +   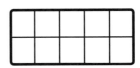   = 19

8   +   5   +   ☐   = 19

The missing number is ☐ .

3 There are 5 red 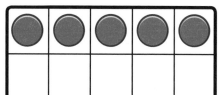, 7 blue 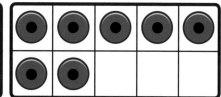 and 5 yellow 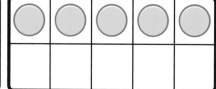 .

How many 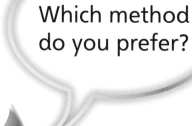 are there in total?

There are ☐ pencils in total.

I can do this by adding 5 + 7 + 5.

I think that using number bonds to 10 helps.

Which method do you prefer?

131

Solving word problems – the bar model ❶

Discover

❶ **a)** Mr Dean has 57 stickers. He buys 30 more.

How many does he have altogether?

b) Mr Dean then puts one sticker in each book.

There are 45 books.

How many stickers are left?

Share

I know part + part = whole, and whole − part = part.

I have used a bar model to represent this. It helps me to see what is going on.

a)

whole

87	
57	30

parts

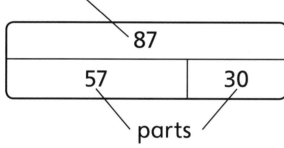

Mr Dean has 87 .

$57 + 30 = 87$

```
  T  O
  5  7
+ 3  0
-------
  8  7
```

b)

87	
45	42

Mr Dean has 42 ☆ left.

$87 - 45 = 42$

```
  T  O
  8  7
- 4  5
-------
  4  2
```

Think together

1 There are 45 pupils in total.

27 are boys. How many are girls?

45	
27	?

There are ☐ girls.

45 ◯ 27 = ☐

T	O
4	5
2	7
☐	☐

◯

2 There are 35 yellow stickers and 16 blue stickers.

How many stickers are there altogether?

?	
?	?

There are ☐ stickers altogether.

35 ◯ 16 = ☐

T	O
3	5
1	6
☐	☐

◯

3 Mrs Bell uses 7 blue stickers, 5 red stickers and 9 yellow stickers.

How many stickers does she use altogether?

We need to work out the whole.

I think there are three parts. Is that possible?

Mrs Bell uses ☐ stickers altogether.

→ **Practice book 2A p97**

Solving word problems – the bar model ❷

Discover

1 **a)** How many marbles are there in the red ⬜ and the yellow ⬭ altogether?

b) Work out the difference between the numbers of marbles in the blue ⬜ and the green ⬜.

Share

I can use two bars to show the different numbers of marbles.

We need to label the bars.

a)

?

24	37
Red	Yellow

```
  T O
  2 4
+ 3 7
  6 1
  1
```

24 + 37 = 61

There are 61 marbles in the red and the yellow altogether.

b) Blue

42

Green

| 17 | ← ? → |

42 − 17 = 25

```
  T O
  ³4̷ ¹2
− 1 7
  2 5
```

There are 25 more marbles in the blue than in the green.

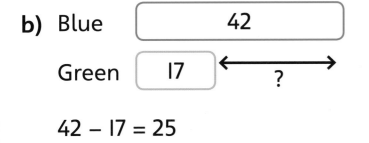

Think together

1 How many marbles are there in the green 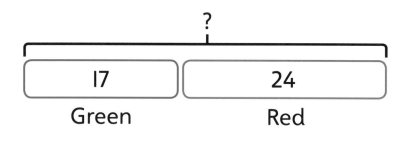 and the

red ⬡ altogether?

?

17	24
Green	Red

17 ◯ 24 = ▢

```
  T  O
   I  7
+  2  4
_____
```

2 The purple has 15 more marbles in it than the blue does.

How many marbles are in the purple ?

Blue | 42 | ← 15 →

Purple | 42 |

?

```
  T  O
  4  2
+ I  5
_____
```

138

3 19 more marbles are added to the green .

How many more marbles are there in the green  than in the red  now?

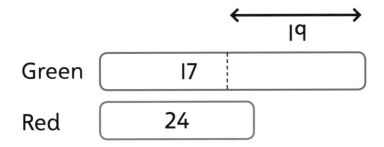

Green [17 ⋮] ←—— 19 ——→

Red [24]

I can see that there are two parts to this question.

I will draw out the information I know, to make it easier!

139

End of unit check

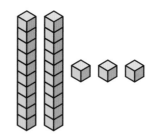

Your teacher will ask you these questions.

1 How many altogether?

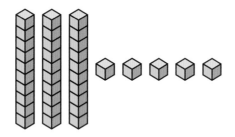

A 85   B 13   C 58   D 40

2 What is the missing number?

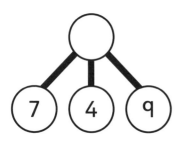

A 749   B 20   C 11   D 13

3 What is the missing number?

50	
32	

A 18   B 82   C 8   D 0

4 Which calculation finds the missing number?

$$17 + \boxed{} = 52$$

A 17 + 52

C 17 − 52

B 52 + 17

D 52 − 17

5 There are 95 children.

Kat has 42 . Tim has 25 .

How many more  do they need so each child can have

one 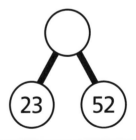 ?

A 77   **B** 53   **C** 88   **D** 28

Think!

Circle the odd one out. Prove it.

$$\boxed{} = 46 + 19$$

37	28

23   52

These words might help you.

ones   tens   exchange

add   subtract   equals

141

→ Practice book 2A p103

Unit 4
Money

In this unit we will ...
- ⚡ Count coins and notes
- ⚡ Compare different amounts of money
- ⚡ Find different ways to make the same amount
- ⚡ Work out the amount of change
- ⚡ Solve two-step problems involving money

Do you remember these coins?

We will need some maths words and symbols. Which have you met before?

pounds (£)   **pence (p)**

coins   **notes**

change

We can use ┤┼┼┼┼┼┼┼┼┼├ 0 1 2 3 4 5 6 7 8 9 10 and [blocks] to help us. How much money is there here?

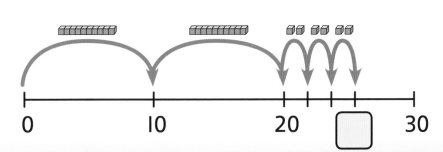

Counting money – coins

Discover

I **a)** How much money is in each tray?

b) Count the money in tray C in a different way.

Key 1p 2p 5p 10p 20p 50p £1 £2

Share

How much is each coin?

a)

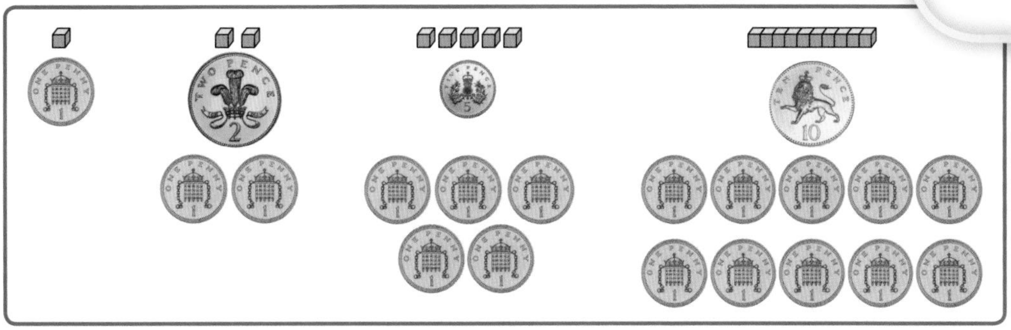

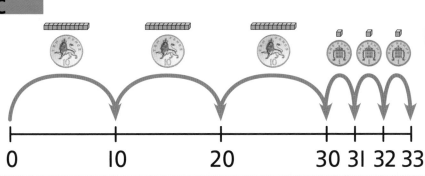

A

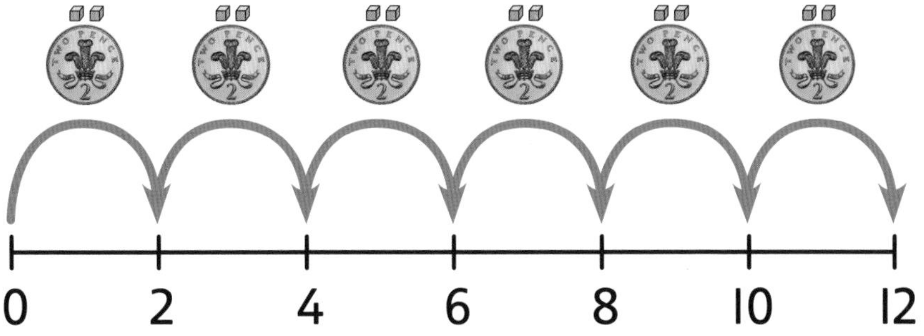

Tray A has 12p.

B

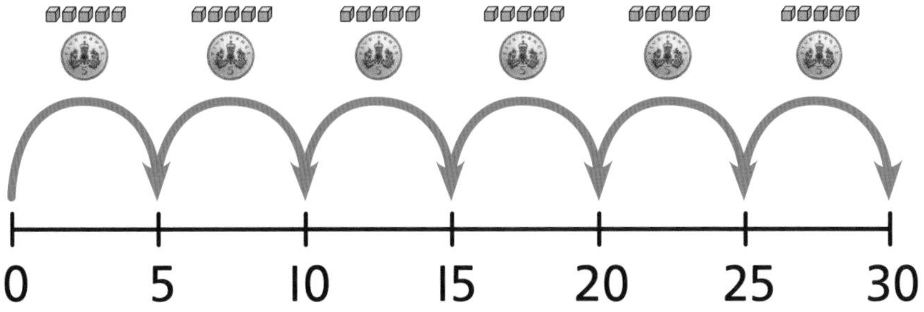

Tray B has 30p.

C

I will count in 10s then in 1s.

Tray C has 33p.

 £5  £10  £20  £50

b)

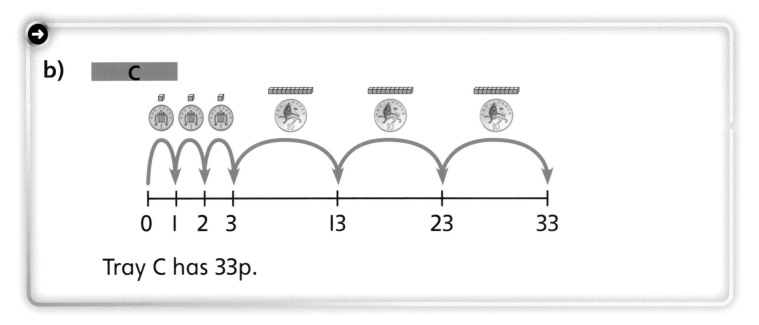

C

Tray C has 33p.

Think together

1 How much money is in the tray?

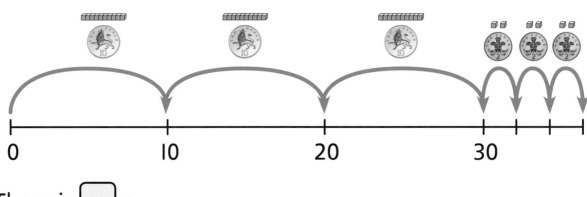

There is ☐p.

Key 1p 2p 5p 10p 20p 50p £1 £2

2 How much money is in this tray?

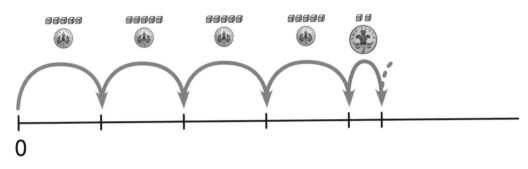

0

There is ☐ p.

---

3 How can you count these amounts?

CHALLENGE

Two 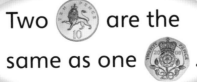 are the same as one .

 £5 £10 £20 £50

→ Practice book 2A p105

Counting money – notes

Discover

1 **a)** How much money has the lady on the stall raised?

b) She is given three .

How much does she have now?

Key 1p 2p 5p 10p 20p 50p £1 £2

Share

a)

> £ means 'pounds'. You write £5 and £10, not 5£ or 10£.

> I will count in tens and fives.
> I will start with the greatest amount.

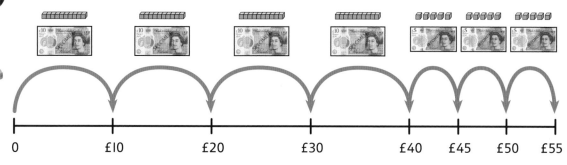

| 0 | £10 | £20 | £30 | £40 | £45 | £50 | £55 |

The lady on the stall has raised £55.

> I could count all the ones in one go.

b)

£55   £56   £57   £58

The lady on the stall now has £58.

Think together

1 How much money is there altogether?

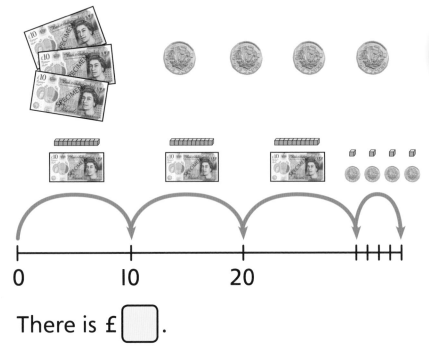

I could have counted in ones.

There is £ ⬚ .

2 How much money has the lady from the stall raised here?

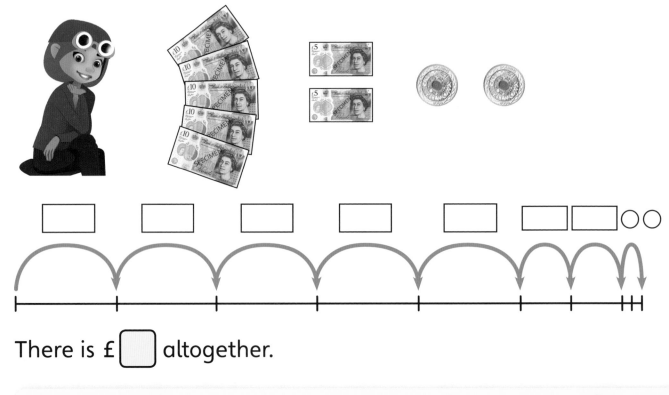

There is £ ⬚ altogether.

Key 1p 2p 5p 10p 20p 50p £1 £2

3 Match the money to the correct total.

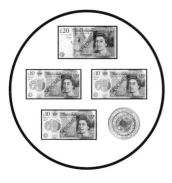

£42

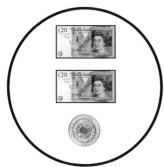

£60

£52

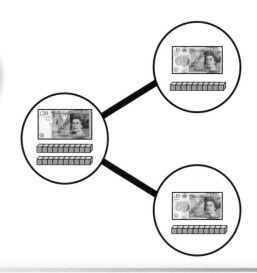

I don't know how to count in 20s! How can I begin?

£20 is the same amount as 2 .

Counting money – coins and notes

Discover

1 **a)** How much money has the girl saved?

b) The girl finds another .

How much money does she have now?

Key 1p 2p 5p 10p 20p 50p £1 £2

Share

a)

I will count all the notes, and then the coins.

I will sort them into pounds and pence so I can count them separately.

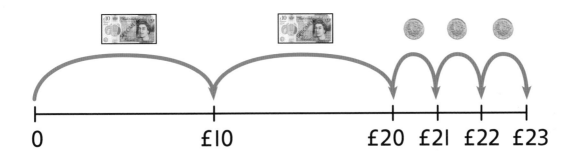

| 0 | £10 | £20 £21 £22 £23 |

There is £23.

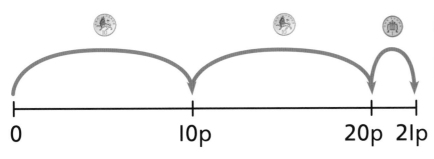

| 0 | 10p | 20p 21p |

There is 21p.

Remember, £1 is the same as 100p.

The girl has saved £23 and 21p.

b)

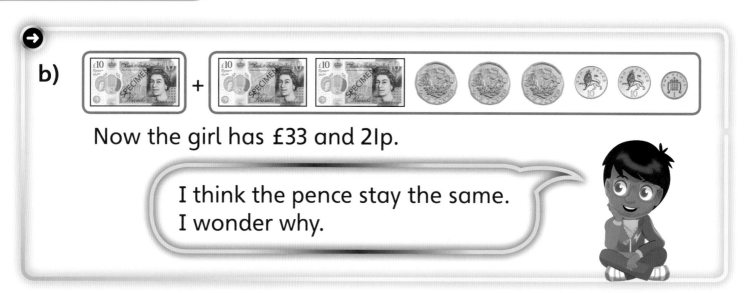

Now the girl has £33 and 21p.

I think the pence stay the same.
I wonder why.

Think together

1 How much is here?

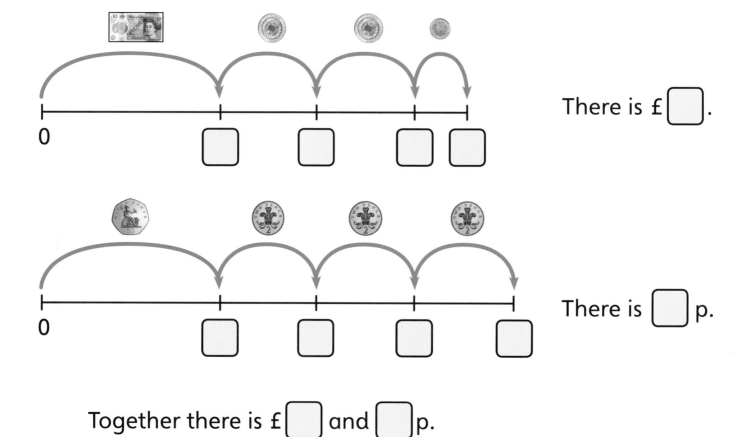

There is £☐.

There is ☐p.

Together there is £☐ and ☐p.

Key 1p 2p 5p 10p 20p 50p £1 £2

2 How much money is there in pounds and pence?

There is £ ⬜.

There is ⬜ p.

Together there is £ ⬜ and ⬜ p.

3 What mistakes has the boy made?

CHALLENGE

I have £10 and 51p.

I will check the pounds first, then the pence.

 £5   £10 £20 £50

→ Practice book 2A p111

Showing equal amounts of money ❶

Discover

❶ **a)** Which of the coins above does Oliver need to pay exactly?

Which of the notes and coins above does Gemma need to pay exactly?

b) When they get home they count what money is left.

How much money do they have left in total?

Key 1p 2p 5p 10p 20p 50p £1 £2

Share

a)

First I will find the parts of 25p.

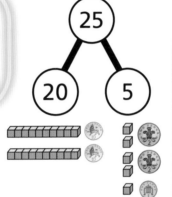

Just pick the coins you need. You might not need all the coins.

Now I need to find coins to match the tens and ones. I do not see enough 1p coins so I will use 2p coins.

Oliver needs  , , .

Gemma needs £8, so I will look at the pounds.

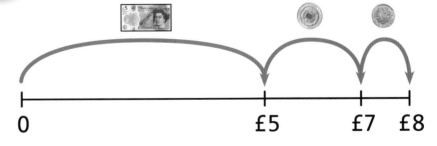

Gemma needs and and .

b)

These are the notes and coins left. They have £11 and 51p in total.

Think together

1 Find the right money to pay for the fruit.

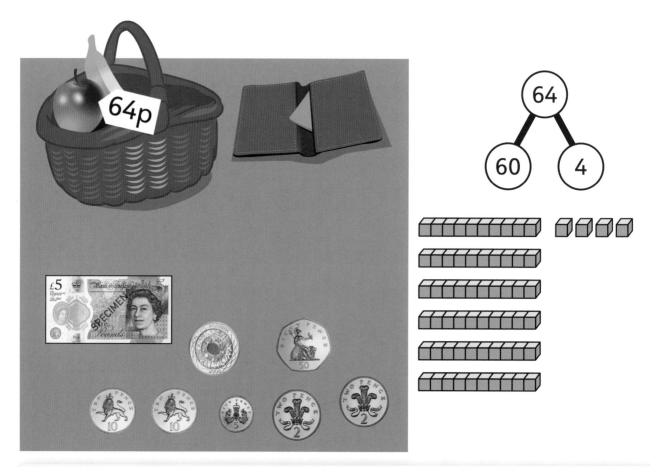

Key 1p 2p 5p 10p 20p 50p £1 £2

2 Choose the right money to pay for the shopping.

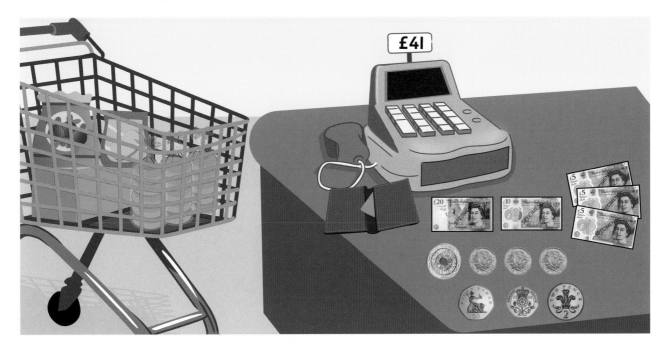

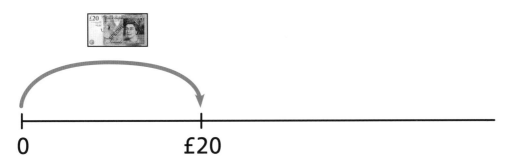

0   £20

CHALLENGE

3 Oliver has exactly £11 and 22p.

Choose coins and notes to give the exact amount.

I wonder which ones I should choose first?

 £5   £10   £20   £50

159

→ Practice book 2A p114

Showing equal amounts of money ❷

Discover

£38

🍦 65p

🥤 75p

🥫 80p

Jenny   Mark

Jenny

Mark

I **a)** Find the right money for each child to get an .

b) Think of another way to make 65p.

Key 1p 2p 5p 10p 20p 50p £1 £2

Share

a)

I think I should start by finding the parts of 65p.

Jenny

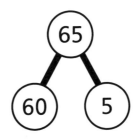

65

60   5

Mark

65

60   5

Jenny can pay with 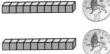 , , .

Mark can pay with 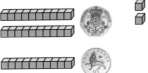 , , , , , .

b)

 + + = 65p

 + + + = 65p

I think there are even more ways.

Think together

1

Paul   Gemma

Gemma

Paul

Paul and Gemma both want a .

Make 75p for each of them.

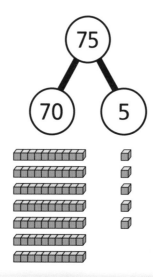

Key 1p 2p 5p 10p 20p 50p £1 £2

2 Find the right money for each person.

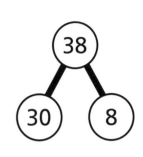

3

Everybody bought a can of drink for 80p.

Find four different ways to make 80p.

CHALLENGE

 £5 £10 £20 £50

163

→ **Practice book 2A p117**

Comparing amounts of money

Discover

Charity Fair

Stall C

Stall A
Money raised

Stall B
Money raised

Stall C

Stall A

Stall B

1 **a)** Did the boy on Stall A or the girl on Stall B raise more money?

b) The girl on Stall C raised more than but less than .

How much could she have raised?

Key 1p 2p 5p 10p 20p 50p £1 £2

Share

I worked out the totals first.

a)

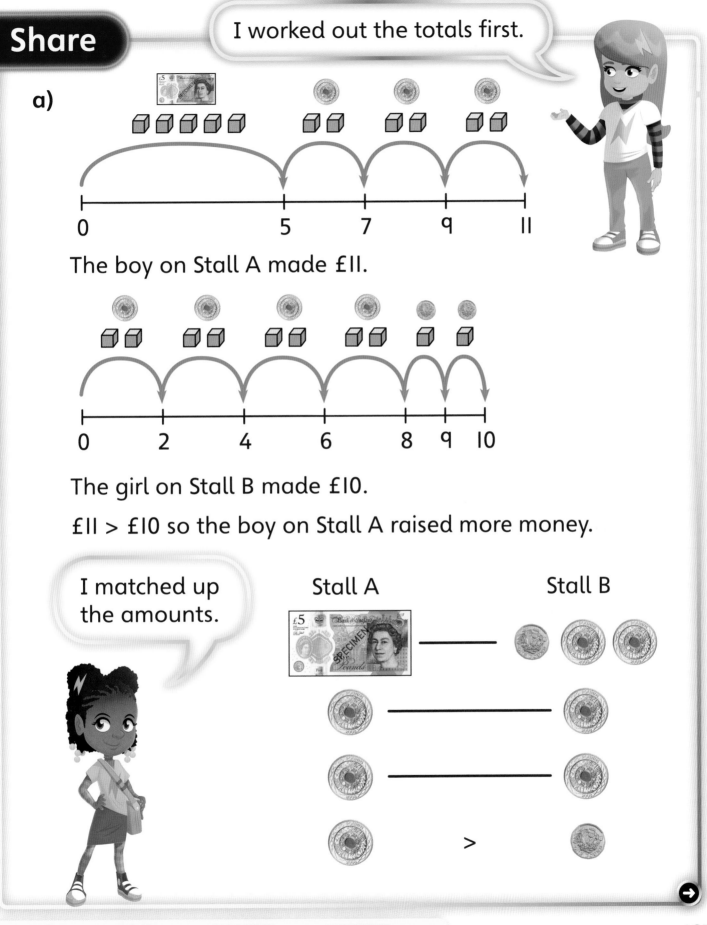

The boy on Stall A made £11.

The girl on Stall B made £10.

£11 > £10 so the boy on Stall A raised more money.

I matched up the amounts.

Stall A   Stall B

>

£5   £10   £20   £50

b) 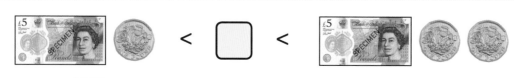 < ☐ <

£6 < ☐ < £9

The girl on Stall C could have raised any amount that is higher than £6 and lower than £9.

Think together

1 Use <, >, or = to compare these amounts.

a)

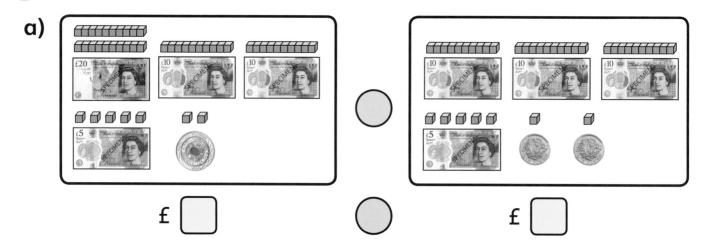

£ ☐ ◯ £ ☐

b)

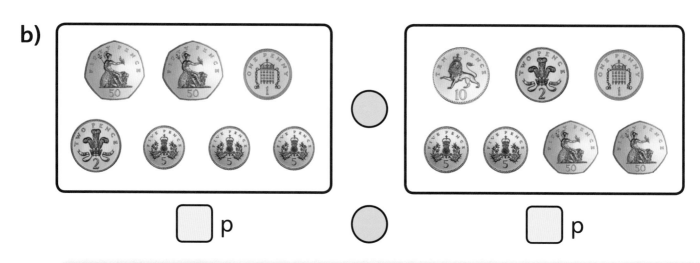

☐ p ◯ ☐ p

Key 1p 2p 5p 10p ⬤ 20p 50p £1 £2

2 Use each of these once to make each statement true.

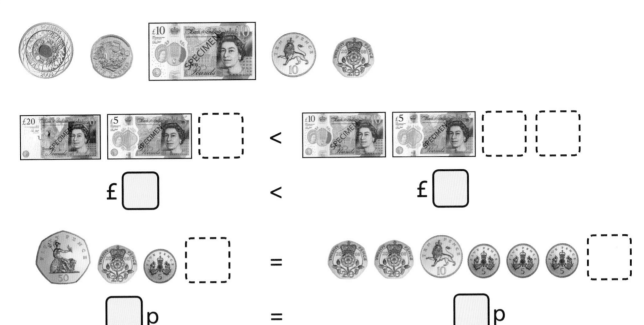

£[ ] < £[ ]

[ ]p = [ ]p

3 Compare these amounts.

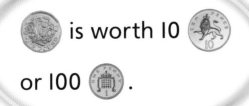 is worth 10 or 100 .

I will compare the pounds first.

 £5 £10 £20 £50

→ Practice book 2A p120

Calculating the total amount

Discover

1 **a)** The girl buys and a .

How much does she spend in total?

b) The boy buys two items. He spends £26.

What does he buy?

168

Key 1p 2p 5p 10p 20p 50p £1 £2

Share

I worked out the money for each item. Then I counted it all.

a)

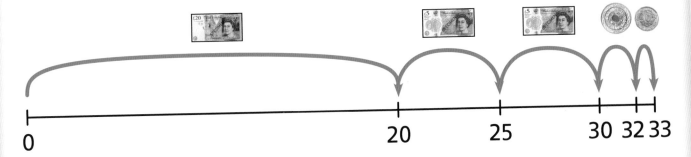

33	
25	8

The girl spends £33 in total.

I used a bar model to show the addition.

b)

26	
18	8

18 + 8 = 18 + 2 + 6 = £26

I tried different additions, until I made £26.

I think I could also use the column method to help me.

The boy buys and  .

 £5   £10   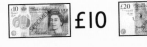 £20   £50

Think together

1 A man buys a  and .

How much does he spend in total?

?	
£40	£18

⬜ + ⬜ = ⬜

He spends ⬜ in total.

2 Marie buys some  for £12.

She also buys some  for £45.

How much does she spend in total?

?	
?	£12

⬜ + ⬜ = ⬜

Marie spends ⬜ in total.

I used notes and coins to make this amount.

Key 1p 2p 5p 10p 20p 50p £1 £2

3 How would you add these amounts?

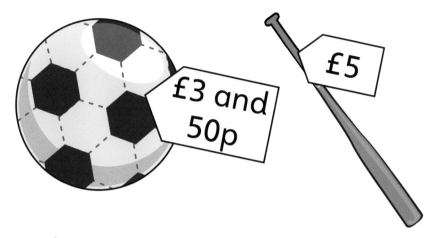

£3 and 50p

£5

and

£2 and 30p

£2 and 50p

Use coins to help you find the totals.

I think I need to add the pounds and the pence separately.

 £5 £10 £20 £50

→ **Practice book 2A p123**

Finding change

Discover

Lucy   Eshan

1 **a)** Eshan wants a . He has .

How much **change** does he get?

b) Lucy has .

How much change would she get if she bought a ?

Key 1p 2p 5p 10p 20p 50p £1 £2

Share

a)

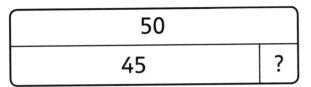

50	
45	?

To find change I need to find the missing part. I can do a subtraction.

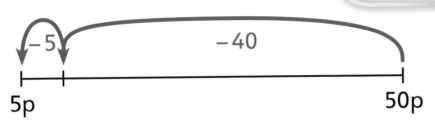

−5 −40

5p   50p

50p − 45p = 5p

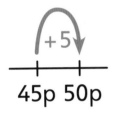

+5

45p 50p

To find change I can use the counting on method to find the difference.

45p + 5p = 50p

50p − 45p = 5p

Eshan gets 5p change.

I remember that £1 is the same as 100p.

b)

+70

30p   100p

30p + 70p = 100p

100p − 30p = 70p

Lucy would get 70p change.

Think together

1 Jamal has 75p. He buys a .

How much money does he have left?

75	
35	

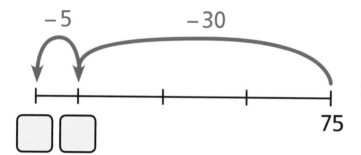

I will check how much  costs first.

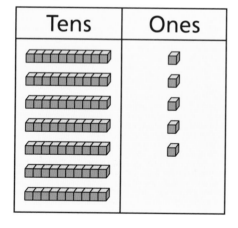

He has ⬜p left.

Key 1p 2p 5p 10p 20p 50p £1 £2

2 Ian was given £35 for his birthday.

Sarah has saved £51.

How much more did Sarah have than Ian?

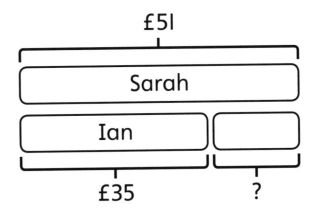

£51

Sarah

Ian

£35   ?

£⬚ – £⬚ = £⬚

Sarah has £⬚ more than Ian.

3 Lesley bought a large ice cream.
Her brother bought a small ice cream.

How much more did Lesley spend than her brother?

Large juice: 45p

Medium juice: 35p

Small juice: 30p

Large: £3 and 50p

Small: £2 and 20p

I will think about the coins to help answer this question.

 £5   £10   £20   £50

→ Practice book 2A p126

Solving two-step word problems

Discover

1 **a)** Cora buys one ⧼ Adult ⧽ and one ⌈ Child ⌉ .

She pays with  .

How much change will she get?

b) Cora buys two 🍿 as well.

How much does she spend in total?

Key 1p 2p 5p 10p 20p 50p £1 £2

Share

a)

I will do this in two steps.

Now I can do the next step.

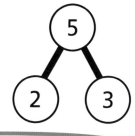

| | 8 | 10 | 13 |

One {Adult} costs £8. One (Child) costs £5.

£8 + £5 = £13

The tickets cost £13 in total.

£20 − £13 = £7

£20		
£8	£5	£7

Cora will get £7 change.

b) The  costs £3. Cora buys two popcorn.

I will show it on a bar model.

£3 + £3 = £6

Two popcorn cost £6 altogether.

Cora spends £13 on tickets.

13 + 6 = 19

Cora spends £19 in total.

Think together

1 Alfie bought one 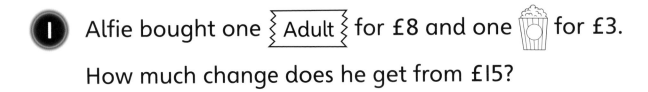 Adult for £8 and one  for £3.

How much change does he get from £15?

?	
£8	£3

First I worked out how much he spent in total.

£⬚ + £⬚ = £⬚.

He spent ⬚ in total.

£15	
?	?

I will put the total Alfie spent into a part in the bottom bar.

⬚ – ⬚ = ⬚.

Alfie gets £⬚ change.

Key 1p 2p 5p 10p 20p 50p £1 £2

2 Jane has . She buys one ⧼ Adult ⧽ for £8 and

two [Child] for £5 each.

Can Jane buy a for £3 too?

⬜ + ⬜ + ⬜ = ⬜

She has spent ⬜ in total.

£20 − ⬜ = ⬜

Jane has ⬜ left so she _____ buy a 🍿 too.

3 James buys a large drink for 🪙 and a small drink.

The small drink costs 🪙 less than the large drink.

How much does James spend in total?

CHALLENGE

⬜ ⬤ ⬜ = ⬜

A small drink costs ⬜

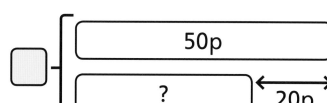

⬜ ⬤ ⬜ = ⬜

James spends ⬜ in total.

End of unit check

Your teacher will ask you these questions.

1 How much money is this?

A £45   **B** 81p   **C** 90p   **D** 45p

2 Which answer shows £9?

A

B

C

D

3 Which answer is equal to   ?

A   **C**

B   **D**

4 Choose the sign to complete the number sentence.

A < **B** > **C** = **D** −

Think!

True or false?

  >

 These words might help you.

pence   equal to

greater than   less than

181

→ Practice book 2A p132

Unit 5
Multiplication and division ❶

In this unit we will …
- ⚡ Decide if groups are equal
- ⚡ Form multiplication sentences
- ⚡ Use arrays
- ⚡ Practise the 2, 5 and 10 times-tables
- ⚡ Solve multiplication word problems

We use these a lot, don't we? You can use a number line for multiplication as well. Can you find 4 × 5 using the number line?

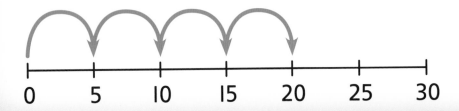

We will need some maths words and symbols. Which of these have you seen before?

equal groups   **multiplication (×)**

times-tables   **times**

We can use an array to help us when we multiply. Can you use 20 counters to make this array? Can you move the counters to make a different array?

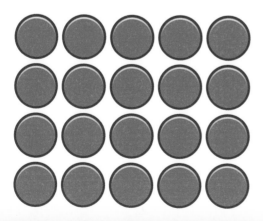

Making equal groups

Discover

I **a)** Are the 🧁 in equal groups?

Are the 🧁 in equal groups?

b) Are the 🍪 in equal groups? How do you know?

Share

a)

There are 2 equal groups of .

Each group contains 6 .

There are 5 equal groups of .

Each group contains 2 .

Each tray is an equal group. Equal groups means there is the same number in each group.

b)

  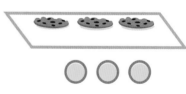

The are not in equal groups.

There are 5 in 2 of the groups and 3 in another group.

These are different groups.

Think together

1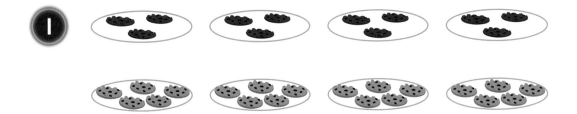

Copy and complete each sentence.

There are 4 groups of ▢ 🍪 .

There are 4 groups of ▢ 🍪 .

2

Copy and complete each sentence.

There are ▢ equal groups of 3 🧁 .

There are ▢ equal groups of ▢ 🍩 .

There are ▢ equal groups of ▢ 🍪 .

3

| James | Hannah |

Who has equal groups?

_____ has equal groups.

Some of the groups don't look the same. I wonder if they still have the same number in them.

187

→ Practice book 2A p134

Multiplication as equal groups

Discover

1 a) 5 chairs fit around each ⬠.

How can you work out the total number of chairs

for 3 ⬠?

b) 2 chairs fit around each ○.

How can you work out the total number of chairs

for 6 ○?

Share

a)

I could add all 3 groups to find the total number of chairs.

There are 3 groups of 5 chairs.

To work out the total, we can write this as 5 + 5 + 5.

This is the same as 3 × 5.

I can do 3 × 5 to get the total. 3 × 5 means that there are 3 groups of 5.

b)

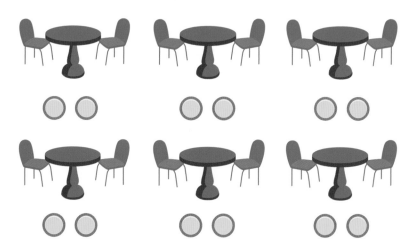

There are 6 groups of 2 chairs.

2 + 2 + 2 + 2 + 2 + 2

6 × 2

Think together

 4 chairs fit around each .

How many chairs fit around 3 ?

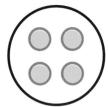 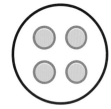 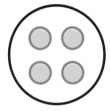

3 groups of 4 chairs

☐ + ☐ + ☐

3 × ☐

2

How many chairs fit around the tables?

Write as an addition and a **multiplication**.

☐ + ☐ + ☐ + ☐

☐ × ☐

3

Henry wrote 4 × 3 to find out how many birds there are.

Is he correct? Explain.

I wonder if the groups need to be the same size for multiplication to help.

→ Practice book 2A p137

Adding equal groups

Discover

1 **a)** How many pieces of white chocolate are there?

b) How many pieces of dark chocolate are there?

Share

a)

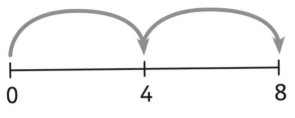

4

4

$4 + 4 = 8$

$2 \times 4 = 8$

There are 8 pieces of white chocolate.

I will use a number line to help me.

b)

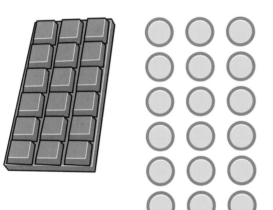

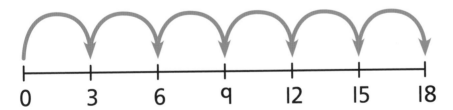

$3 + 3 + 3 + 3 + 3 + 3 = 18$

$6 \times 3 = 18$

There are 18 pieces of dark chocolate.

There are 6 groups of 3. You could add the 6 groups together or use multiplication.

Think together

1 How many muffins are there?

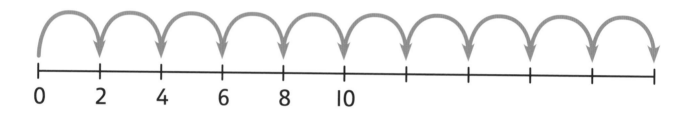

0   2   4   6   8   10

2 + 2 + 2 + 2 + 2 + 2 + 2 + 2 + 2 + 2 = ☐

10 × 2 = ☐

Are all the groups equal?

I will count how many groups there are.

2 How many apples are there in total?

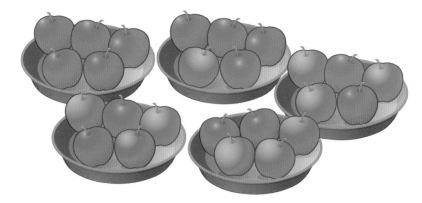

0

5 + 5 + 5 + 5 + 5 = ⬜

5 × 5 = ⬜

What does each 5 represent?

3 I had 5 baskets of 5 apples. I now have one more basket of 5 apples. How many apples are there now?

CHALLENGE

⬜ + ⬜ + ⬜ + ⬜ + ⬜ + ⬜ = ⬜

⬜ × ⬜ = ⬜

I wonder if there is a quicker way than addition.

195

Multiplication sentences

Discover

1 **a)** How much has been collected in 5p coins?

b) Danny writes 3 × 2.

What row of the table does this calculation represent?

What do the 3 and the 2 represent?

Share

I will start by adding together the right number of 5s.

I will look at the table to find the right information.

a)

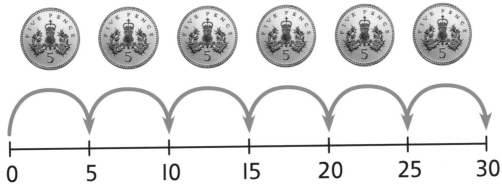

5 + 5 + 5 + 5 + 5 + 5 = 30

6 × 5 = 30

30p has been collected.

b) There are 2 kinds of coin with a 2: the coin and

the coin.

3 × 2 means 3 groups of 2. There are 3 .

The 3 is the number of coins. The 2 represents the .

Think together

1

Some friends bought 5 🍦 and 3 🎂.

How much did they spend on each?

They spent £ ⬚ on 🍦.

⬚ × £ ⬚ = £ ⬚ .

They spent £ ⬚ on 🎂.

⬚ × £ ⬚ = £ ⬚ .

2. Use counters to show these multiplication sentences.

3 × 2 ◯◯ ◯◯ ◯◯

4 × 3 ●●● (

5 × 5 (

3.

Look at the picture. Tell a story of 4 × 2.

Can you think of another story to tell?

First, I will think about what things I can see in twos.

→ Practice book 2A p143

Using arrays

Discover

I **a)** How many 🫙 did Ali bake in total?

How did you work out the answer?

b) How many 🫙 did Ed bake in total?

Did he bake more than Ali?

Share

a)

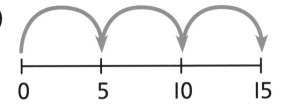

$5 + 5 + 5 = 15$

$3 \times 5 = 15$

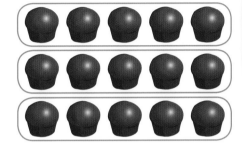

Ali baked 15 in total.

> I know that 3 rows of 5 means 3×5.

b)

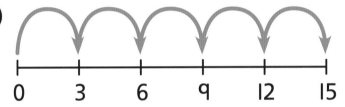

$3 + 3 + 3 + 3 + 3 = 15$

$5 \times 3 = 15$

$3 \times 5 = 15$

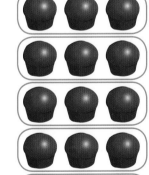

> I think 3×5 gives the same answer as 5×3.

Ali baked 15 in total.

Ed and Ali baked the same number of .

Think together

1 **a)** Here are some counters in a 6 × 2 array.

How many counters are there?

Show how to work it out in two ways.

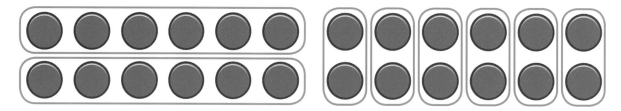

☐ + ☐ = ☐   ☐ + ☐ + ☐ + ☐ + ☐ + ☐ = ☐

☐ × ☐ = ☐   ☐ × ☐ = ☐

b) The cakes are ordered in a 10 × 5 array.

How many cakes are there?

Show two ways of working it out.

☐ × ☐ = ☐

☐ × ☐ = ☐

When objects are arranged in rows and columns like this, they are called arrays. You can find the total by adding the amount in the rows or the columns.

2 Complete the number sentences to find the total number of dots.

4 + 4 + 4 + 4 + 4 = 20

◻ × ◻ = ◻

5 + 5 + 5 + 5 = ◻

◻ × ◻ = ◻

CHALLENGE

3 Show a 5 × 2 array in two different ways.

Show the groups in rows.

Show the groups in columns.

How many different additions and multiplications can you find?

I wonder how many different calculations I can make!

203

→ Practice book 2A p146

2 times-table

Discover

1 **a)** How many ice cubes are needed for 3 🥛 ?

  b) How many ice cubes are needed for 8 🥛 ?

Share

a)

$2 + 2 + 2 = 6$

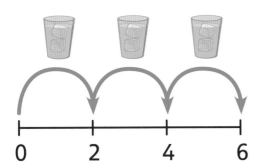

0   2   4   6

$3 \times 2 = 6$

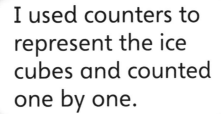
I used counters to represent the ice cubes and counted one by one.

I counted in twos.

b) $2 + 2 + 2 + 2 + 2 + 2 + 2 + 2 = 16$

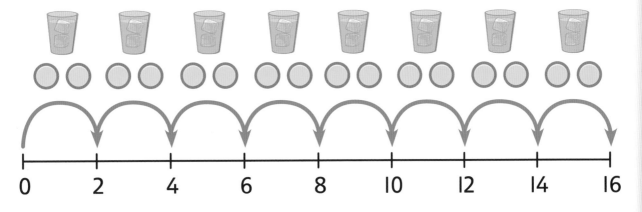

0   2   4   6   8   10   12   14   16

$8 \times 2 = 16$

I used a number line to help me work out the answer.

205

Think together

1

2 ice cubes for each glass

How many ice cubes are needed for 9 ?

2 + 2 + 2 + 2 + 2 + 2 + 2 + 2 + 2 = ☐

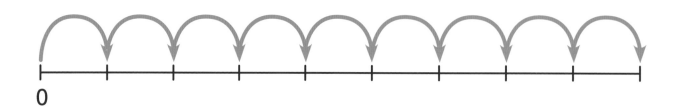

0

9 × 2 = ☐

2 How many ice cubes are needed for 10 ?

```
├──┼──┼──┼──┼──┼──┼──┼──┼──┼──┤
0
```

2 + 2 + 2 + 2 + 2 + 2 + 2 + 2 + 2 + 2 = ☐

10 × 2 = ☐

> For every 1 glass more, 2 more ice cubes are needed.

3 a) How many ice cubes are needed for 11 ?

11 × 2 = ☐

CHALLENGE

b) How many ice cubes are needed for 12  ?

12 × 2 = ☐

> I could count in twos from 0, or I could add on from the tenth glass.

207

→ Practice book 2A p149

5 times-table

Discover

Each player needs a bottle of water.

1 The coach needs to give each child 1 🍼 .

a) How many 🍼 does the coach need?

b) A new team of 5 children arrives.

How many 🍼 does the coach need now?

Share

a)

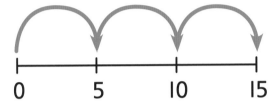

I will count the players one by one.

$5 + 5 + 5 = 15$

$3 \times 5 = 15$

15 bottles of water are needed.

I think it will be quicker to count in fives.

b)

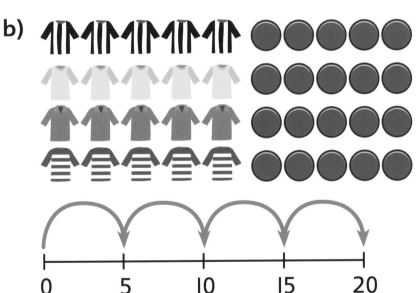

$5 + 5 + 5 + 5 = 20$

$4 \times 5 = 20$

20 bottles of water are needed.

209

Think together

1 Complete the multiplication.

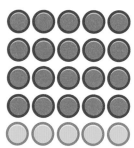

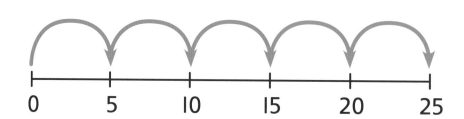

$5 \times 5 = \boxed{}$

2 Copy and complete the diagrams and number sentences.

a)

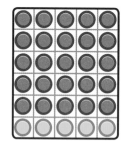

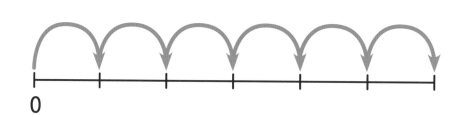

0

$\boxed{} \times 5 = \boxed{}$

b)

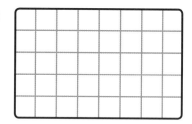

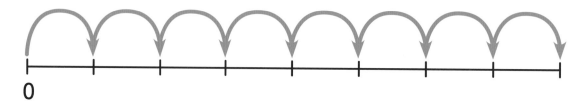

0

$\boxed{} \times \boxed{} = \boxed{}$

3 Copy and complete the number sentences.

CHALLENGE

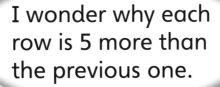

I wonder why each row is 5 more than the previous one.

$1 \times 5 =$ ☐

$2 \times 5 =$ ☐

$3 \times 5 =$ ☐

$4 \times 5 =$ ☐

$5 \times 5 =$ ☐

$6 \times 5 =$ ☐

$7 \times 5 =$ ☐

$8 \times 5 =$ ☐

$9 \times 5 =$ ☐

$10 \times 5 =$ ☐

$11 \times 5 =$ ☐

$12 \times 5 =$ ☐

211

→ Practice book 2A p152

10 times-table

Discover

1 **a)** How many stickers are there on 3 sheets?

b) Jamal has 6 sheets of stickers.

How many stickers does he have in total?

Share

I can count in 10s.

a)

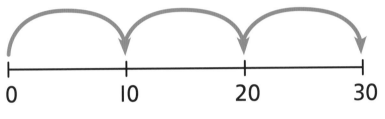

$10 + 10 + 10 = 30$

$3 \times 10 = 30$

There are 30 stickers on 3 sheets.

I wonder if I can use multiplication to help.

b)

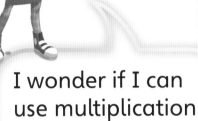

10
20
30
40
50
60

$10 + 10 + 10 + 10 + 10 + 10 = 60$

$6 \times 10 = 60$

Jamal has 60 stickers in total.

There are 10 in each group.
There are 6 groups.

Think together

 There are 10 stickers on 1 sheet.

How many stickers are there on 7 sheets?

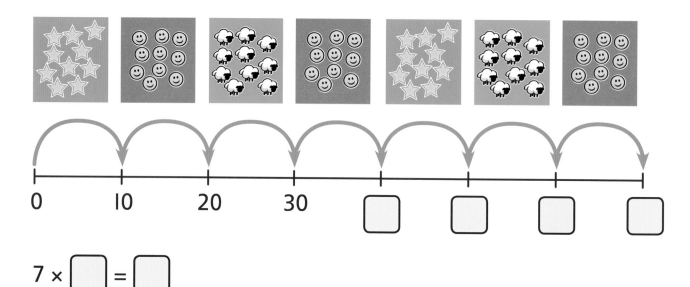

0   10   20   30   ☐   ☐   ☐   ☐

7 × ☐ = ☐

2 There are 10 stickers on 1 sheet.

a) How many stickers are there on 8 sheets?

0 ───────────────────

8 × 10 = ☐

b) How many stickers are there on 9 sheets?

0 ───────────────────

9 × 10 = ☐

c) How many stickers are there on 10 sheets?

0 ───────────────────

10 × 10 = ☐

3 Copy and complete the number sentences.

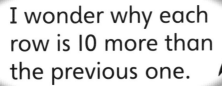

I wonder why each row is 10 more than the previous one.

$1 \times 10 = \boxed{}$

$2 \times 10 = \boxed{}$

$3 \times 10 = \boxed{}$

$4 \times 10 = \boxed{}$

$5 \times 10 = \boxed{}$

$6 \times 10 = \boxed{}$

$7 \times 10 = \boxed{}$

$8 \times 10 = \boxed{}$

$9 \times 10 = \boxed{}$

$10 \times 10 = \boxed{}$

$11 \times 10 = \boxed{}$

$12 \times 10 = \boxed{}$

215

→ Practice book 2A p155

Solving word problems – multiplication

Discover

Once upon a time, there was a prince and princess. The princess was 2 times as tall as the prince.

The king was 5 times as tall as the prince!

1 **a)** Use a  to represent the prince.

How many do you need to represent the princess?

b) The king is 5 **times** as tall as the prince.

How many do you need to represent the king?

Share

a)

First, I will think carefully about what '2 times' means.

The princess is 2 times the prince's height.

If I represents the prince,

$2 \times 1 = 2$

2 represent the princess.

I wonder if I can use multiplication to help.

b)

The king is 5 times the prince's height.

$5 \times 1 = 5$

I need 5 to represent the king.

Think together

1 Use the forecast to help you answer each question.

Monday	Tuesday	Wednesday	Thursday	Friday	Saturday	Sunday
☀	🌧	☁	🌧	☁	☁	☁

a) Complete the weather chart.

☀	🌧	☁
1 day	☐ days	☐ days

b) Complete the sentences.

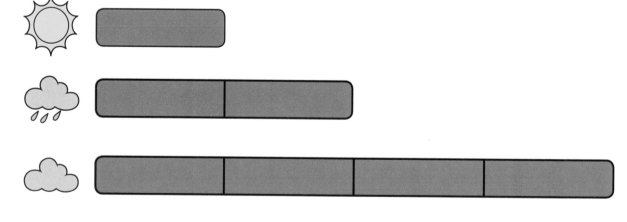

There are ☐ times as many days of 🌧 as ☀.

There are ☐ times as many days of ☁ as 🌧.

2 Complete the sentence.

There are ⬜ times as many ⬤ as ◯ .

---

3 A dragon is 2 times as tall as the king.

If the king is 5  tall, how tall is the dragon?

CHALLENGE

The dragon is ⬜  tall.

I could use blocks to help
with these calculations.

219

→ Practice book 2A p158

End of unit check

Your teacher will ask you these questions.

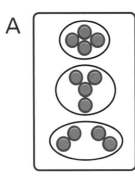

1 Which shows equal groups?

A   B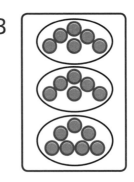

A None   B A   C B   D Both

2 Which addition matches this multiplication?

5 × 4

A 5 + 5 + 5 + 5 + 5   C 5 + 4

B 4 + 4 + 4 + 4   D 4 + 4 + 4 + 4 + 4

3 Which calculation matches this array?

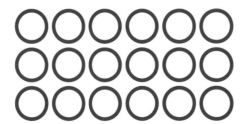

A 3 + 3 + 3   C × 2

B 3 × 6   D 6 + 6 + 6 + 6 + 6 + 6

4 Which card completes this number sentence?

$$7 \bigcirc \square < 15$$

5 Which is longer?

| A | 5 | 5 | 5 | 5 | 5 | 5 |

| B | 10 | 10 | 10 |

A A

C They are equal

B B

D You cannot tell

Think!

25   12   50   15   28   13   30   14

Ajay says, 'Only one of these numbers is in both the 2 times-table and the 5 times-table.'

Is his statement true or false? Convince me.

These words might help you.

digit   count   times-table

ones   tens   multiply

→ Practice book 2A p161

What do we know now?

Can you do all these things?

⚡ Work with numbers up to 100
⚡ Add and subtract within 100
⚡ Count money and work out how much change you need
⚡ Start to use multiplication

It's ok to make mistakes as long as you try again!

Now you're ready for the next books!

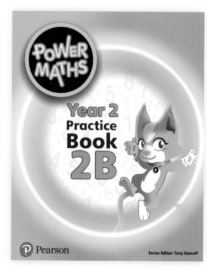